All at Sea

Libby Purves, who edited this book for the RNLI, is a professional journalist and broadcaster but only an amateur sailor. With her husband Paul Heiney and one-year-old son Nicholas she sails the yacht *Barnacle Goose* off the British and Irish coastlines, without, so far, any need of the lifeboats.

All at Sea

True and tall tales
trawled by
Libby Purves

Fontana Paperbacks

First published by Fontana Paperbacks 1984

Set in Linotron Plantin
Made and printed in Great Britain by
Richard Clay (The Chaucer Press), Bungay, Suffolk

Contents

Foreword

by His Grace the Duke of Atholl,
Chairman of the Royal National Lifeboat Institution

As Chairman of the Royal National Lifeboat Institution I am delighted to introduce this book of anecdotes which is being published to celebrate the RNLI's 160th anniversary. Here is a selection of salty tales, many true experiences and, I suspect, a few tall stories. All have been donated by the contributors, and well-known cartoonists have provided illustrations free of charge so that the royalties can be donated to the RNLI. Libby Purves kindly agreed to edit the book for us and took a great personal interest in every stage of its production, spending a considerable time sifting through the diverse contributions. The Institution is indeed grateful to receive such support, as it faces the continual challenge of building and maintaining the finest possible lifeboats for its volunteer crews. In buying the book, you are helping with their humanitarian work which, in the 160 years since the RNLI was founded, has resulted in over 110,000 lives being saved from certain death at sea. I hope you will enjoy the book and will recommend it to your friends.

RNLI Acknowledgements

All the stories in this book have been donated by the authors, to whom the RNLI owes grateful thanks. Unfortunately it was not possible to include every story due to the magnificent response.

Thanks are also due to the following publishers who have kindly waived payments: Granada Publishing, Hodder & Stoughton, Hutchinson Publishing Group, Martin Secker & Warburg, and William Collins.

The cartoonists have also donated their illustrations and we are particularly grateful to Geoffrey Dickinson and his colleagues on *Punch*, and to Mike Peyton.

The original idea for the book came from Mrs Belinda Braithwaite, an RNLI supporter in Warwickshire.

The manuscript was sub-edited by Ray Kipling and Edward Wake-Walker and was typed by Hilary Dewing, Rosalind Smalley and Olive Walker.

Introduction
by Libby Purves

'It may seem odd', wrote the Bishop of Southwell, 'for a bishop to admit to a criminal offence even if it was committed over forty years ago . . .' and went on to detail a story of purloined brass cannon, crates wrapped in old pieces of marquee, and suspicious labels reading MEDICAL STORES. In a way, it did seem odd; but after a long, enchanting ramble through the rest of the contributions to this book, the Bishop's youthful misdemeanour barely raised an eyebrow.

Where else, between two covers, would you expect to learn about Sir Alec Guinness's taste in camouflage paint, Lord Longford's early religious confusion while on parade at Dartmouth, Donald Sinden's adventures with enormous tough Wrens, and Robert Morley's little unpleasantness in a lock-basin? What other volume brings together the story of how an octopus shot at Edward de Bono with a harpoon-gun, the account of how James Herriot saved a cargo of sheep bound for Russia, and a glimpse of the ferociously yachty childhood which made Ewen Southby Tailyour the man he is (and the man who single-handedly charted the Falkland Islands)? Where else will you discover why Lulu toured Canada with a black eye after her one boating experiment, and why distressed mariners may well be rescued on occasion by an entire lifeboat crew dressed up as giant greenfly? Odder things happen at sea than mere cannon-thefts by future bishops.

When the RNLI asked me to edit this book for their 160th anniversary, I leapt at the chance. For one thing, it seemed a good opportunity to do something for the lifeboat service without having to stand in the rain rattling a tin, or to struggle dangerously under the limbo-bar at the Kensington Lifeboat Dance while a steel band called Hugo and the Hugonotes banged what sounded like a collection of old anchors. After these previous harrowing experiences, I was only too pleased to live vicariously for a week or so, reading through the contributions to *All at Sea*.

As always happens – whether one is standing in the street with a sou'wester and tin, demanding sponsorship for a five-year-old's determined totter around three laps of a public park, or running a bazaar stall – the response to the call has been remarkably generous. Admirals, authors and politicians, comedians and churchmen and cricketers, came promptly back when we wrote to them, with stories hilarious and horrifying and, in some cases, pretty dirty. The lifeboat coxswains and hon. secs. weighed in with some stories of their own, most of which I believe; and distinguished MPs, chairmen of shipping companies and editors of dignified journals took the time to remember and type out their best after-dinner nauticalia. The whole community of those who use the sea – for fishing, for naval or merchant marines, for yachting or for cruising across – has contributed freely to the book: so have many who only dream about the sea, or dread it, or remember it from long ago.

Even the refusals were illuminating and full of goodwill. Stirling Moss would have helped, only he 'dislikes beaches because of the sand'; John Arlott declares himself an 'abject landlubber', and Geoffrey Boycott is terrified lest 'my contact lenses float away'. Ned Sherrin claims to have barely been to sea, 'let alone survived an *anecdote*', and Melvyn Bragg wrote with manly frankness:

I swim but I don't sail. Once I went on a yacht off the coast of Brittany. We capsized and I swam a registered three miles back to land. That is my only experience of doing something so stupid as being in a boat on the water when I could be in an aeroplane above the water.

12

But the goodwill was there, as it always is. Once again, the lifeboats have been done proud. Writers and cartoonists have given their services freely, because on dark and wild nights, year after year, lifeboatmen have given far more. They will continue to do so; every penny that we can raise to buy equipment, boats and gear for them will make the dangerous coasts of Britain and Ireland a better place for those who venture out to sea.

Liner Types

Pursers, passengers and purple passages

PEYTON

Sir Robin Gillett

Former Lord Mayor of London;
Elder Brother, Trinity House

A purser was reprimanding a new bedroom steward: 'I have had a complaint from the young lady in cabin A20 that you burst in on her when she was taking a bath. What have you to say for yourself?'

'Well, it was like this, sir. I went in to change the towels thinking the cabin was empty – the bathroom door was not locked – and there she was in the bath.'

'So, what did you do?'

'I said, "Sorry, madam," and shut the door again quick.'

'My lad,' said the purser, 'in a situation like that you have to learn to use tact. First, you should have knocked, then, if you had entered as you describe, you should have said, "Sorry, sir," to let her think you hadn't seen that much.'

A few days later the purser saw the steward with a black eye.

'What on earth have you been up to now?' he demanded.

'Well, sir, it's you and your tact. I took the honeymoon couple in A35 their morning tea and they was . . . they was in bed together, sir. So I put down the tray as if nothing was happening and, remembering what you said about tact, I asked, "Which of you two gentlemen likes sugar?"'

Sir Hugh Casson
President, Royal Academy

November, mid-Atlantic. A force eight gale and the *QE2* is hove to, grey waves leap fifty feet to slap viciously at the lounge windows, tea is being, with difficulty, served.

After a particularly dramatic lunch, accompanied by crockery crashes and stewards' curses from the pantry, my neighbour – an elderly lady – rises unsteadily to her feet. 'I think,' she said, 'I'll go and sit on the *other* side of the room. It looks as if it would be calmer there.'

Captain C.R. Kelso
Chief Marine Superintendent, Cayzer, Irvine Shipping Ltd

A Southampton-based passenger liner was completing her annual drydocking and we were gathered in the ship's office for a meeting with the repair contractors to discuss progress and check the repair lists. The ship manager, a man of few words from the north-east coast, was in the chair and each of us waited to comment on the ravages inflicted upon our particular part of the ship by his workforce. The door opened and 'Taff' came in bearing a tray of tea. As he was preparing to leave, the ship manager grabbed him by the arm, gave him a pound note and said, 'Taff, nip over to the docks shop and get me twenty Senior Service – if they haven't got Senior Service, get me something else.' Taff disappeared and the meeting continued.

Some ten minutes elapsed and Taff reappeared. He waited until the chairman gave him his undivided attention, then placed a meat pie, a bar of chocolate and forty pence in front of him with the words, 'They didn't have no Senior Service.'

Robin Ray
Broadcaster and entertainer

A cannibal, on a voyage on the *QE2*, went into the restaurant for lunch. The head waiter gave him the menu. 'This is no good to me,' said the cannibal. 'Bring me the passenger list!'

Captain Ian Gibb
General Manager (Fleet) P&O Cruises

As a sixteen-year-old cadet aboard the newly commissioned *Arcadia* in the early 1950s I found myself frequently taking passengers around the bridge for tours of inspection of all the most up-to-date navigational aids.

During the latter part of one of these tours, I had occasion to observe that one particular gentleman was showing great interest in the radar, and when the majority of the other passengers had left I went over to him to explain more fully the complexities of the instrument. I praised this modern marvel, tracing its development and the technical know-how which had made its contribution to the war effort so valuable. From a sixteen-year-old, you can imagine my enthusiasm if not my full expertise!

My passenger was smiling but he let me have my say and waited until I had completely exhausted my knowledge. Then he announced in a Scots accent, 'Och, very good laddie . . . but of course, you know, I invented it!'

It was Sir Robert Watson Watt, I was later informed.

* * *

One of our regular female passengers was known as 'an officer eater' and she selected a young officer for sacrificial slaughter on each of her cruises. It was not unknown for an officer to be repatriated at the end of one of these cruises with quite serious spinal problems! At a party in the wardroom on one cruise it became obvious to me that I was being 'set up' by my fellow officers as the victim, and I was manoeuvred into a corner where I became the target of this infamous lady. During the hubbub and noise I was finally able to duck away and bolted for my cabin, hotly pursued by the lady in question and also half of the wardroom, to see the fun. Fortunately I got to my cabin in time – but then, to my horror, found that my door had been removed from its hinges in preparation. It's no use trying to slam a curtain. Curtains!!

Dr Ronald Hope
Director, Marine Society

The Irish passenger arrived fuming at the purser's bureau.

'Sir,' he said, 'I would have you know that the hot water in the taps is cold, and furthermore that there is none of it.'

*   *   *

'Is it always foggy about here, captain?' asked the lady passenger as the ship was off the Newfoundland Banks.

'How the devil should I know, madam?' the captain replied testily. 'I don't live here.'

Ted Dexter
Former England Cricket Captain

In 1962, I was elected captain of the MCC Touring Party – as it was then known – to visit Australia. The journey was made by air to Aden and then on the SS *Canberra* to Perth. Life aboard luxury liners can be fattening and it was reported to me that a previous touring party had averaged an extra stone apiece on arrival down under!

By chance the famous distance runner, Gordon Pirie, was also on board and it seemed a useful opportunity to follow his ideas on keeping trim. These consisted of standard stretching exercises for mobility, coupled with a few minutes' running round the deck to keep the legs in tone.

It was the second part of the schedule to which fiery Fred Trueman took exception: 'I've just bowled a thousand overs for Yorkshire and England, and I need a rest – not a keep fit course.' Amateur Captain Dexter was being taken to task for over-enthusiasm by the great professional fast bowler.

I still have home movies of the boys pounding round the deck in the Indian Ocean, with Brian Statham, Len Coldwell and Barry Knight, my other key quickies, very much in evidence.

Now nobody can say with certainty that one thing always leads to another. But the fact is that it was Frederick Sewards Trueman who was absent for a match or two with a bad back, while Statham, Coldwell, Dexter and Knight never missed a day!

Basil Boothroyd
Writer and broadcaster

Stay off the captain's table. He usually does after the first few meals and you can't blame him. This leaves you with the rest of the unsparkling company. They wonder how you got to be there. You wonder how they did. You wonder how you did, if it comes to that.

Our company was a minor botanist, an ex-mayor of a Mid-lands town and his ex-mayoress, a very shy spinster lady of title and an elderly archdeacon fancying himself as a mildly risqué raconteur. None of them the sort, my wife said, that you would choose to be trapped in a lift with. They felt the same about us. Or so we felt. No open coolness, you understand. In fact the erstwhile mayor was inexorably sociable each night after dinner, insisting on brandies for four in the lounge, never failing to say, as he raised his glass, 'It burns up the contents of the stomach!'

The day we were to dock at Tilbury at nine in the morning I had a lunch date in London and could see that the inevitable confusions and delays of disembarking were going to make it a close thing. My wife suggested that we ask the captain to get us off quick. This being the last night, even he hadn't felt able to abandon us. I wasn't keen. This was a man with nearly a quarter of a mile of ship to look after. But I steeled myself and put it to him. He said to leave it with him, but his tone didn't sound too dependable.

A misjudgement on my part. We were still sleeping at six the next morning when white-coated stewards entered the cabin in force to collect the bags. We got up and packed at speed. Three and a quarter hours later we were first in the customs shed. And alone. No sign of a customs man, even.

When one finally emerged from a secret hidey-hole, buttoning his uniform jacket and dashing drops of tea from his lips, we were glad to see him. This feeling was not reciprocated. He had a sour, interrupted look and it was plain, even before his command to open everything up, that he had marked us down from afar as a pair of rich and over-privileged berks who had pulled golden strings to hit English soil while their late shipmates were fighting for a footing in the gangways.

He knew how to cut our sort down to size. Everything wasn't only taken out, but shaken out. We tried to help him with the sponge-bag zips. He waved us off. We swore there was nothing dutiable in the hairbrushes. He went off to a good light, rattling them. He submitted gobs of toothpaste to secret tests. Perused the paperbacks for porn. He was in no hurry.

By this time the waiting boat-train was filling with our old shipmates, streaming aboard by the hundred and never a bag opened. It finally pulled out, while our man was still demanding a receipt for the camera we bought two years before in Guildford.

A bad time. It hadn't been made better by passing waves from the mayor, mayoress and botanist, though at least the lady of title didn't see our dirty laundry being chucked back at us: the archdeacon, from his roguish look, was telling her one of his stories. And it's my guess that it probably pointed less of a moral than this one.

Which is stay off the captain's table. As I think I said at the beginning.

Dr Ronald Hope
Director, Marine Society

In the days of £ s d (pounds, shillings and pence) one baffled citizen of the United States asked at the bank on board the *Queen Elizabeth*, 'How much do I have to give you in American money to get ten dollars-worth of your money?'

Another passenger, a lady, asked, 'What is the rate of exchange for pounds today?' On being told, she replied, 'Thank you. I have no idea what it means but my husband told me always to ask the rate.'

* * *

It was the occasion of the ship's concert aboard a large passenger ship crossing the Atlantic and the captain was present supporting the organizer. The ship was running before a high sea on the quarter but behaving well. An eminent lady singer was in the middle of a song when the officer of the watch sighted a light ahead and had to alter course a few points to avoid it. Without warning, the ship took a violent lurch. Within seconds the audience, the singer, the ten-piece orchestra, about two hundred chairs and tables, plus innumerable glasses and coffee cups, were all thrown in a confused heap on the starboard side of the main lounge. For a few moments it looked as though there might be a panic, but the captain rose to the occasion. Picking up the diva, he persuaded her to return to the platform, where he bade her hang on to the grand piano which, fortunately, was firmly secured to the deck. Then, calling for silence, he said, 'Ladies and gentlemen, there is no cause for alarm. Furthermore, I would like to add that in the whole of my career at sea I have never seen an audience so moved by a performance as we have been moved by this lady's singing tonight.' And without more ado, he disappeared in the direction of the bridge to see exactly what had happened.

David Coulson

Deputy Head of Advertising Control,
Independent Broadcasting Authority

In days of yore, when there were such things as British passenger liner fleets on regular schedules to the rest of the world, I was a purser. It was my company's policy to encourage officers to mix with passengers (up to a point!) and, to that end, we each had an assigned table of eight in the first class dining saloon.

The first dinner down-Channel was a pretty predictable affair. Introductions over, one's passengers would hunt around for conversational topics and naturally felt the need to ask 'their' officer questions.

Q: How many passengers are aboard?

A: About 1400 but until we've finished checking all the tickets collected at the gangway, we're not entirely sure.

Q: Which one's the captain?

A: He's not in the saloon tonight, but that's his table over there.

Q: What's our first port of call?

A: Gibraltar, but nobody goes ashore.

Q: How far away's the nearest land?

A: About half to three-quarters of a mile.

Q: What, France – over there? *(pointing to port)*

A: No, down there. *(pointing to the sea bed)*

Alan Whicker
Television broadcaster and writer

I considered travel in all its forms in my autobiography, *Within Whicker's World* – quite predictably! We had just filmed a series aboard the *QE2*, where sea travel has reached its most spacious and, far from the airlines' expensive excess-baggage nightmare, you can take more luggage than you'll ever need right round the world without paying another penny or having to pack or unpack.

A couple in a nearby stateroom took full advantage of this facility. They arrived on board with a remarkable array of cabin trunks. 'We thought they were for the ship's shop,' said a steward.

Then they went ashore at every port of call and bought a mass of hefty souvenirs – Balinese ebony statues, Thai teak furniture, Chinese carpets, Japanese sound systems, Rajasthani chests. . . . Their overflowing double cabin was jammed deck to ceiling with crates and they could only just squeeze into one of its two beds, tucked away in a corner. She told me it was the first time they'd slept together for years.

Some women will do anything to go shopping . . .

Sir Robin Gillett

Former Lord Mayor of London;
Elder Brother, Trinity House

It was a glorious, star-studded night when a passenger on the boat deck stopped a passing sailor and enquired as to the name of one very bright star.

Paddy, for it was he, said he didn't know but would consult the officer of the watch, from whom he received the following fulsome information to convey back to the passenger.

'Tell him,' said the OOW, 'that it is Sirius, it is in the constellation of Orion and it is the brightest star in the firmament.'

Back comes Paddy to the boat deck. 'Sor, I have it now: it's the constipation of O'Brien, it's serious and it's the tightest arse in the infirmary.'

* * *

The reputation of sailors and their baser appetites dies hard, it seems.

Some years ago, when cruising the West Indies as staff commander of the *Empress of Britain*, I took the rare opportunity to go ashore for a look around with one of the other officers.

Dressed in 'civvies', we landed with a boatload of our passengers at the quay in Port of Spain, Trinidad. The usual touts swarmed around us offering taxi drives to places of interest. As we walked off they followed us down the street despite our continual protestations that we did not require their services.

It dawned on me that they mistook us for passengers, so by way of clarification I said, 'Look, we don't want a taxi, we are not passengers, we are members of the crew.'

Understanding swept instantly over their smiling black faces as they cried, 'Ah, you want a woman!'

Captain Robin Woodall
Master, *Cunard Princess*

Some tales of the sea can hardly be believed. This one is true. It happened to me!

The captain of a cruise ship in north-west Alaskan waters when doing his rounds meets little old lady on deck. She said to the captain, 'Oh captain, the air up here is so beautifully clear and clean. What altitude are we?'

Slightly bemused, the captain looked over the side and replied, 'Well, about sixty feet above sea level, madam.'

*   *   *

It was a typical grey North Atlantic on that summer's day in 1972. The sky was the usual sullen overcast and *QE2* was homeward bound from New York with a moderate breeze and swell from astern, pushing 28½ knots through fair visibility of six miles or so in light rain.

As the senior watchkeeper on the 12 – 4 watch I was enjoying a peaceful afternoon. The bridge was quiet except for the sound of the sea, the clicking of the gyros and the whir and hum of the radars. Suddenly the intercom from the captain's cabin buzzed. This in itself was unusual, but what was to follow was even more so. 'Hand over to your watchmate and come to my cabin,' was the order. There I found the senior officers of the ship in conference, together with one of the pursers working on the company's private codebook. I was informed that the ship was being held to ransom for a large sum of money by a man in Brooklyn, New York, who stated that there was a bomb on board, and that this would be detonated by his accomplices on the ship, who had nothing to lose if the ship sank. Her Majesty's Government took the threat seriously enough to send out a bomb disposal team to the ship in mid-Atlantic, and I was to pick them up.

So it was that some hours later I found myself in charge of one of the ship's launches, lurching over the grey swell, a couple of miles away from *QE2*. At this point I did wonder what we were doing out there. If the great ship went bang we were a long way from home, but then the Irish doctor with us reminded me that land was only 2½ miles away – straight down!

The disposal team was parachuting from an RAF Hercules, and their minimum drop height was 250 feet, so with a cloud level of 200 feet, in theory they could not jump, but they felt as they had come this far it seemed a shame to go home again. Thus it was that the first I saw of them was their legs appearing through the mists of the overcast sky as they swayed slowly to the sea.

Back alongside the massive dark grey steel wall of the ship we were slowly hoisted up the eighty feet to the boatdeck, to be met by a battery of cameras, as by now the passengers had got the buzz. Once secure at deck level I escorted the bomb team to the bridge, where again the senior officers were gathered. Understandably, all at this stage were looking a little tense.

Wondering what to do at this point, I introduced the captain to the leader of the team, who was standing dripping in his black wet suit. He slowly undid the front of it and pushed his hand inside. Pulling out a *Daily Telegraph*, he said to the captain, 'I don't suppose you have read this morning's paper, sir?'

Lord Mancroft
Former Deputy Chairman and Managing Director
of the Cunard Line

I was on the bridge of *QE2* when she was edging her way alongside pier 92 in New York harbour with several feet of ice in the harbour but no tugs to hand and no longshoremen to man the ropes. They were all on strike.

Captain Warwick decided to take *QE2* in singlehanded, with a few Cunard head office clerks and typists on the ropes. (This had been done before, but it takes skill. The Italian Line once pushed their *Leonardo da Vinci* halfway up Fifty-second Street and into a Puerto Rican supermarket.)

Warwick waved the pilot aside and after sixty minutes of unassisted ice-breaking (which is thirty more than is needed with assistance) we were safely tied up alongside.

I thought the pilot looked a little out of countenance and suggested that Warwick might offer him a consoling word.

'Anything I can do for you, pilot?' he asked, without much warmth.

I thought there was going to be an explosion. But no.

'Yes, captain, there is,' said the pilot. 'I would like a signed copy of the log for my grandchildren.'

Lynne Reid Banks
Author

This story is not really mine, but my mother's.

It happened in the summer of 1940. Hitler's invasion was expected. My mother, my cousin and I were being evacuated to Canada. One mighty liner with her burden of English children had already gone to the bottom. Only after terrible soul-searching had it been decided in the family that the risk was worthwhile.

My cousin and I were equipped with life-jackets, which we had to wear at all times, and suede pouches, lined with oilskin, containing our documents, which we wore round our necks. We had not yet begun to realize what our long exile would involve. To us it was a great adventure. We spent the days running round the ship getting in everyone's way, alternating, in my case, with bouts of seasickness. I was sick (I kept count) nine times the first day, three the second, none the third.

On the third night out, when we had been put to bed, my mother, ever a claustrophobic, ventured up on deck for a breath of air. The ship, of course, was blacked out. The convoy which had accompanied us part of the way had either scattered or was invisible. My mother felt acutely the loneliness of the ship on the open sea, the menace lurking under it, its terrible vulnerability. . . .

A crew member approached her as she stood at the rail. 'You shouldn't be up here, madam,' he said.

'I couldn't bear it below,' she said.

'If anything were to happen, you ought to be with your children.'

She felt a pang of guilt and turned to go back to our cabin. Suddenly the sailor stiffened. My mother turned back towards the rail. And she saw it – the bubble-trail in the starlight, as a torpedo rushed towards us.

She knew at that moment that our leaving England had been a terrible error. In that advancing menace she saw an omen – not death now (she saw almost at once that it was wide of its mark) but the death of the heart later. Instead of seeing her past life in a flash, she seemed to see the future – long years of separation from the people she loved, in their hour of trial; an ordeal by loneliness, humiliation and isolation for herself as a penniless, dependent refugee; years more, in the future, adjusting to whatever radical changes the war would wreak on our family, our country – and the world.

The torpedo sliced under the stern and was gone.

'Did you see it?' the sailor muttered. 'Swine nearly got us!'

'I could almost wish it had,' my mother said. Then she shook off her fear and came back down to our stuffy cabin to make sure we were all right.

Dr Ronald Hope
Director, Marine Society

'Do you ever feel homesick, captain?' the lady passenger asked sympathetically.

'Madam, I am never home long enough,' came the reply.

Run for Your Lifeboat!

RNLIkely tales

David Thomas
Honorary Secretary, New Quay Lifeboat Station

It was a beautiful sunny day and the tide was full in when the farmer arrived on the sea front at New Quay. He had been told that if he paddled in the sea his rheumatism would be cured. He took off his shoes and socks, turned up his trousers and spent about half an hour enjoying himself at the water's edge.

A few of the local longshoremen were sitting on the pier, and after coming out of the sea the farmer spoke to them and explained that he felt a hundred per cent better and that he would be able to run up the hill with no effort.

'Do you think I could take back a bottle of sea water to the farm with me?'

'Oh yes,' they said, 'just give us half a crown and help yourself.'

Back down the pier he went, filled his bottle and went home happy.

A month later he came back to New Quay again. It was a spring tide and the sea had gone out a considerable distance. The same longshoremen were sitting on the pier and the farmer could hardly believe his eyes.

'Well, well,' he said to them, 'you have sold a lot of sea water since I was here last month.'

Eric W. Bancroft

Honorary Secretary, Tenby Lifeboat Station

During the summer, lifeboats are often called out to rubber dinghies which are blown out to sea. At Tenby, the normal practice on picking up a casualty is to ask from which beach they have been blown out – North Beach, Castle Beach or South Beach. In August 1981, the inflatable lifeboat was launched on one of these incidents and on reaching the casualty the helmsman asked, as usual, 'Where have you come from?'

'Manchester,' was the reply.

* * *

Tenby's inflatable lifeboat was called to rescue a young lady being blown out to sea in an inflatable dinghy. On arriving, the crew asked her why she was so far out without any paddles or a life jacket. The lady, who was on her honeymoon, informed the crew that she was sitting in the dinghy on the water's edge so that her husband could take her photograph. He had said, 'You are a bit too close,' and pushed the dinghy out with his foot. The wind and tide did the rest.

* * *

Tenby lifeboat station is situated off the Castle Hill but right in the town. However, on a low tide the area below the lifeboat house is a very pleasant secluded beach. During one of the fine

38

spells in the summer of 1981 an urgent call for the assistance of the lifeboat was received early one evening. The maroons were fired and within minutes a few hundred people descended on to the Castle Hill to watch the launch. The view became even more spectacular when they were rewarded with the sight of four terrified nudists desperately scrambling for their clothes.

Dick Evans
Former Coxswain, Moelfre Lifeboat

My first rescue after being appointed coxswain of the Moelfre lifeboat was a most unusual one. The wife of the then honorary secretary of the lifeboat telephoned me to say that she had received an urgent telephone message from the RSPCA: a cow had fallen over the cliffs near Point Lynas near Amlwch. I was instructed to launch the lifeboat and proceed to give assistance.

As it was a Saturday night my regular crew were not available and I decided to launch with three grammar school boys, two elderly retired seamen and the mechanic. I also took the boarding boat with me as I realized it could be useful.

On arriving at Point Lynas I found the cow under steep cliffs with its front legs on a ridge. Rocks were protruding all around so I was unable to take the lifeboat close to the scene. I had a 100-fathom rope on the lifeboat; I tied one end to the lifeboat and put the three boys in the boarding boat, two of them to row the boat, and the third to pay out the rope. They managed to tie the rope around the neck of the cow and the rest of the crew pulled the cow slowly towards the lifeboat.

It was a fine clear evening and I could see about a hundred Anglesey farmers on top of the cliff watching the whole operation. I distinctly heard one of them say, 'The b..... fool is going to drown her.' They evidently thought I was going to tow the cow at a considerable distance from the lifeboat, whereas my intention was to get the cow alongside the lifeboat. The poor animal was in a very bad way, having been in the water for six hours.

After extreme difficulty we eventually managed to lash the cow to the side of the lifeboat, and by means of corks and a line ensured that her head was kept above water while the lifeboat proceeded very slowly to a safe point on a nearby sandy beach. The cow managed to walk ashore where the owner took charge of her.

The amazing thing is what happened afterwards. In two weeks' time the cow calved (after being in the water, remember, for six solid hours), and approximately twelve months later that same calf was awarded a champion's prize at the London Smithfield Show.

The animal's owner paid all the lifeboat's expenses and gave a generous donation to the RNLI. I received a very nice letter of thanks from the RSPCA and also a Thanks on Vellum from the RNLI which is now hanging in the Moelfre Lifeboat Station.

The Right Reverend Peter Mumford
Bishop of Truro

My recurring problem is seasickness.

My first vicar took me on an extended interview to the Channel Islands and found his earnest would-be curate reading a book called *The Blessedness of Giving*. As we sat together on deck, that was precisely what I was doing – into the sea. Oddly, I was still given the job.

My wife is prepared to swear that when we undertook a similar trip together, she caught me reading *The Times* upside down. That was certainly how *I* felt.

On both occasions I remember praying fervently for total shipwreck, without benefit of rescue, even by the RNLI!

Ray Kipling
Public Relations Officer, RNLI

One of the most tedious tasks for lifeboatmen is a search in fog. During one such search, for a man overboard from a vessel in the English Channel, there was very little information as the lifeboat launched. The coxswain was therefore pleased to hear the radio crackle into life as the coastguard called up with more details.

'The man you are looking for is wearing a red anorak, blue jeans and is of medium build and height.'

The coxswain turned to the crew, 'Thank goodness for that description – I'd hate to pick up the wrong one!'

At Harwich the lifeboat crew enter a float in the town carnival every year and try to pick a topical subject for their entry. One summer there had been a plague of greenfly in the area, so the crew dressed up in green tights, vests and tied-on gauze wings. In the middle of the procession the maroons exploded and their lorry raced to the lifeboat station. The crew had no other clothes to change into, so they set off in their weird garb. The missing fisherman, who had been adrift for some hours, was so surprised to be rescued by six greenfly that he thought exposure had affected the balance of his mind!

* * *

The radio ship *Mi Amigo,* home of the pirate radio station Radio Caroline, caused a number of lifeboat calls during the 1960s and 1970s, and most of the Essex lifeboats had been out to her assistance. It was therefore something of a mixed blessing when in March 1980 it was learned that she was dragging her anchor and was in danger of running aground.

This time it was the turn of the Sheerness lifeboat which launched into a force nine gale and found the *Mi Amigo* rolling and pitching heavily, shipping heavy seas and unable to start her pumps. The ship was on a sandbank so the seas were very confused as Coxswain Charles Bowry drove the lifeboat towards the casualty. With great skill and courage he made thirteen approaches to take off the four survivors safely, and he was awarded the RNLI's silver medal for his gallantry. However, the coxswain's own account of the rescue makes little mention of the dangers.

'It was no time to wishy-washy about. The name of the game was to get alongside. You have got hold of the wheel, you know, and after a while, as she's coming off the top of a sea and starting to jump down, you can feel your old hands tightening up waiting for the crunch. When it doesn't happen you think, "Well, that can't be bad. We got away with that." The seas were all peaking up, just like a load of bell tents all around the boat. We did a bit of parleying about whether he should bring off his belongings. I said, "I will now show you why we shouldn't take your gear off." One minute we were down below looking at his rudder, his prop and about fifteen feet along his skeg, the next minute my lads, who are now up on the bow, are looking down at him. So he said, "I see what you mean." Then he said to me, "Can I bring a bird on board?" I turned to the lads, who grinned and nodded in agreement, so I said, "Have you got a woman on there?" He said, "No, it's a canary!" Never mind a medal from the RNLI – I reckon we should have had one from the RSPCA.'

John Corin
Penlee and Penzance Branch, RNLI

Long ago it was decided at a Cornish lifeboat station, which shall be nameless, that a certain amount of first aid instruction should be given to the crew. The local doctor was recruited and thought fit to begin with the subject of artificial respiration.

'Now, my man, what is your first action on finding a person apparently drowned?'

'Sarch 'is pockots, cap'n.'

Patrick Howarth
Author and former Public Relations Officer, RNLI

The first time I ever went out on service on a lifeboat was at Peterhead, possibly the coldest place in Britain. I had just finished lunch when I heard the maroons fired. I dashed to the lifeboathouse and found the crew already on board, fully kitted out.

I asked the coxswain if I could come too and he agreed. He told me that there was an injured seaman on board a trawler and we were taking a doctor out to him.

I told the coxswain I was very impressed by the speed with which the crew had assembled. He asked me to report on this when I returned to London. The coxswain then gave suitable orders, the lifeboat went down the slipway and put to sea.

I think it was about two minutes later when the coxswain turned to me and said, 'We have forgotten the bloody doctor.'

Billy Burrell
Coxswain, Aldeburgh Lifeboat

During the war, our lifeboat was called out to a Lancaster bomber whose engines had broken down. The Lancaster had glided into the water and her tail had broken off. It was a dark night and as we reached the bomber the coxswain asked me to go aboard her to search the cockpit and fuselage for survivors. The airmen were either dead or had bailed out, so I went back to the lifeboat. I had just stepped aboard to report to the coxswain when the lifeboat started lifting upwards, almost clear of the sea. We found that we had driven over the submerged port wing of the aircraft. As the starboard wing started to fill with water and, therefore, to sink, the port wing was lifting up, pushing us out of the water. Fortunately, before we went any higher, the port wing also started to fill and we were quietly returned to our normal place in the water. I'm sure it was the only time that the Aldeburgh lifeboat has been airborne.

* * *

I joined the lifeboat crew as soon as I was old enough, being a local fisherman, so I have seen some strange rescues in my time. During the war years, Suffolk was pretty much in the front line and there were restrictions on all ship movements, including the lifeboat. One night we were called out to a tanker which was on fire, and to reach her we unwittingly passed out of our designated area. The tanker was part of a convoy going north from the Thames and up the north-east coast, and when we got alongside her an officer asked us to pick up a pump from another ship in the convoy and ferry it across to the tanker. This was quite a task as no ships could show lights and we had to winch the heavy pump down on to our deck then hoist it on to the tanker. They got the fire under control and offered us some coffee and sandwiches which were lowered down to us in a bucket.

We were very pleased for the refreshments and as we lay alongside the tanker we did not notice the approach of an armed trawler whose skipper had seen the shadow of the lifeboat against the tanker's side and, assuming it to be a U-boat, decided to ram us. The lifeboat was suddenly thrown violently upwards, breaking our masts. When we pulled ourselves together we realized that one crew member was missing. Imagine our surprise when we found him sitting quite happily on the deck of the tanker, still eating his sandwiches. He had been catapulted out of the lifeboat and, he proudly told us, had landed without spilling a drop of his coffee.

* * *

The Aldeburgh lifeboat had been called out to help a converted cabin cruiser which was in difficulties in a southerly gale. On board was a young man who pleaded with our coxswain to save his boat, as he had spent a lot of time and money converting her. The coxswain agreed to try and help, so he took the young man aboard the lifeboat and sent me and another lifeboatman on to the cabin cruiser. We secured a tow-rope to the capstan on the foredeck and signalled to the lifeboat. We had only gone a few hundred yards when the whole capstan was wrenched clear of the deck and went over the bows.

The lifeboat circled round, passed the tow again and this time we fixed the rope round the cleats in the mast. The towing went well for half an hour when suddenly the foremast, tabernacle and tow-rope were wrenched out and disappeared over the bows.

Again the lifeboat circled round to bring the tow-rope back to us on the cruiser. There was not a lot left on deck to secure the tow, so we used the hatch coaming. We caught a big sea, there was a crash and away it went. We were determined not to give up. This time I was going to make sure nothing got carried away, so I took the tow-rope through the hatch into the engine room and made it fast to the engine. The tow held and we made for Lowestoft harbour.

As we approached the harbour, there was a heavy swell. A big sea caught the cabin cruiser and snapped the tow-rope. We veered off and hit the sea wall. My colleague and I managed to scramble back on to the lifeboat just as the cabin cruiser broke up and sank, right in the entrance to the harbour. At least we tried!

Jimmy Savile
Television and radio personality

For many years I have been proud to be an honorary crew member of the Beaumaris lifeboat. When I appeared at the International Boat Show at Earls Court some time ago it was wonderful to be able to invite the entire crew to back me up on that splendid occasion. Fun we have had in plenty, like the time I was doing a television film of our boat being launched for a call.

The Beaumaris boat lives at the top of a steep concrete slipway and access to the sea is started by all the crew climbing aboard, then one shore-based person strikes a large knob with a heavy hammer. This releases a shackle and the whole she-bang plunges into the sea.

So that the camera would know when the boat was due to speed from its covered shelter, we all shouted, 'Five, four, three, two, one,' whereupon the hammer would belabour the knob, with the camera rolling because of the shouted count-down. Unfortunately, such was the excitement that the man wielding the hammer counted down to one with the rest of us, then forgot to strike the blow!

The skipper turned round as in slow motion, with all of us

ın a state of shock because we were still in the garage, and he said, 'Hit the bloody peg, man.'

'Ahhh . . .' hollowed our team member, dealt the peg a blow and out rushed several tons of lifeboat, nearly decapitating a cameraman who had poked his head over the concrete slipway and almost received his come-uppance from tons of briny-bound lifeboat.

Keith Hopkins
Navigator/Radio Operator, Yarmouth Lifeboat

Dave Kennett, our coxswain, in his everyday job as local garage-owner sometimes finds himself doing a lifeboatman's job on land. One foggy night an elderly couple had broken down in their car and Dave was called out to tow them back to his garage.

On the return journey he had reached some traffic lights and was waiting for them to change when his girlfriend drove up out of the fog in her car and shouted to him, 'Lifeboat.' To get to the quay as quickly as possible he swapped cars with her without having time to explain about the elderly couple in tow.

Having got to the lifeboathouse and having fired the first maroon (two are fired to summon the crew), he was amazed to see his girlfriend arrive towing only a short piece of ragged rope.

'Where's the car?' he shouted.

'What car?' she asked. 'I'm sitting in it.'

'Not that one, the other one!'

She was totally perplexed; in her excitement and eagerness

48

to see the lifeboat go out she hadn't noticed the old people and had accelerated away, snapping the tow-rope and speeding to the boathouse alone.

So while the lifeboat set out on her search in the fog, a land search party was sent out to discover a bewildered pair of pensioners still sitting in their car at the traffic lights.

Bill Beavis
Yachting journalist

They knew a thing or two when they made me lifeboat crew *reserve*; during the entire six months we lived near the station I never once got there in time. I blame two factors: one, our house was outside the village at the bottom of a very steep hill; and two, instead of a car like everyone else, I only had a bike.

The fact that I would never go out in the lifeboat didn't stop me thinking that I might. And during this period I lived in a state of suspended animation, worried even about taking my clothes off at night. I was also very careful where I went. I didn't want an emergency catching me in the loft, or at the end of a very long ladder, or lounging in the bath. I developed an animal-like reaction to noise, always listening for the sound of maroons. Never in my life have I remained so tensed, so alert. Once when a lorry backfired I cleared cloth, plates and cutlery from a candlelit dinner.

The first call-out I missed was the morning after the Hockey Club dance. Too many drinks, rhumbas and hokey-kokeys must have dulled my finely honed edge. My wife had to put me to bed. At 3 a.m. the maroons went off above the village. BOOM! BOOM! I thought they had gone off under the bed.

'Quick!' I shouted. 'What have you done with my clothes?' A lazy arm arced slowly across the bed and deposited my bow tie and dicky.

Outside, the bike was propped ready by the shed. I felt the tyres, they were good and hard; with my sleeve I wiped the rain off the saddle. I tried my flying start, it was something I had been practising. But something went terribly wrong and instead of landing on the seat I forked down on the crossbar.

'What are you doing rolling about on the lawn?' asked a voice I recognized but could not see, her torch focused on my pupils.

'I can't go, I'm hurt badly.'

'But you must go,' she said, pointing the torch out across the wind-driven sea. 'There is somebody out there depending on you.'

'Oh *sod* them,' I gasped, but the traditions of the lifeboats are instilled into every Englishman who lives by the sea and somehow I dragged myself up off the grass.

Cycling towards the village I could see stabs of car head-lights illuminating the houses. Then occasionally the screech of tyres as another of the lifeboat's crew drove through the empty streets towards the harbour. Here and there a bathroom light could be seen and babies heard crying. Dogs disturbed by the sound continued now, barking in conversation. One dog I recognized lay quietly inside his gate waiting for his master to return. Would he ever return, I wondered. Would any of us?

I returned about five minutes later, the lifeboat had already left. I felt disgraced like a schoolboy; at that moment, missing the lifeboat seemed the most awful thing in the world. It was a feeling I would get used to. My wife would have gone back to bed and my main thought now was to get home quickly and reassure her that I was safe; we had only been married a year. I leaned the bike by the side of the shed ready for the next emergency and cooed softly through the letter box. Well, give her time to dry her eyes, I thought, when she failed to come tripping down the passage immediately. Ten minutes passed and I moved around to our bedroom window with a handful of gravel from the path. Little stones chipping against the window pane have romantic memories for us. But not this night obviously. I rang the bell, I hammered the door, I woke next door's chickens. None of these things aroused her.

Half a mile down the road there was a public telephone. A loud ringing alongside the bed would do the trick. The operator was very kind. I explained I was a lifeboatman with no small change; I didn't go into too much detail. She said she could ring the number. Finally, after what seemed an age, I heard my wife answer and the operator begin to speak.

'Will you accept a reverse-charge call from Yarmouth?' she asked.

'At four o'clock in the *morning*? Certainly not!' Then it clicked and the line went dead.

After that I always took my front-door key.

Lord Killanin
Former President, International Olympic Committee

A few years ago I was visiting the lifeboat station at Galway Bay, together with the then inspector of lifeboats. After the official duties we retired to a local hostelry. The Aran lifeboat at that time had an honorary medical officer who was a lady. She joined us in drinking our pints, and on looking at my clock I realized that the normal licensing hours were well past.

'I wonder whether we should be careful about breaking the licensing laws in case the sergeant decides to check that everyone is law-abiding?'

'That is impossible,' said one of the crew.

'Why?' I asked.

To which I received the reply, 'He is married to the doctor and is at home baby-sitting.'

John Corin
Penlee and Penzance Branch, RNLI

One fine day, many years ago, an old coaster had the misfortune to lose her propeller off Newquay. The mate was despatched ashore in the ship's boat to telegraph for a tug to come from Hayle. Watchers ashore, seeing the boat come away from a vessel which had no obvious cause to anchor, assumed that in some way life was in imminent danger. The lifeboat was summoned and for some reason it could not be launched down the slip, then the steepest in the country. The boat was therefore taken on the carriage normally used to return it from the harbour, through the town and down to the shore. In the process it twice slid off the carriage, to the fury and confusion of all hands. Eventually it was hastily launched and with no wind the crew sweated at the oars to reach the ship anchored quite some way off. On arriving they found the master leaning calmly and contentedly on the rail, nursing a large mug of tea. He looked at them with some surprise and interest and addressed the cox'n thus: 'Some pretty lil' boat you got there, cap'n, come far 'ave 'ee?' The cox'n's reply is not recorded.

David Aubrey
Honorary Secretary, Port Talbot Lifeboat Station

Fishguard Pryce was the one regular who stood out like a sore thumb in the seafaring regulars of the old Dock Hotel: the only man in a gang of old salts and young ones who was not wanted. They were all friends since boyhood, caring, sharing, shipmates to the end, all except Fishguard Pryce – liar, cheat, gambler, brawler, drunk, wife-beater and father of eight children, all bearing the brand of his temper. One man alone could handle Pryce, Sergeant Jenkins, a giant of a man, a noted boxer and a man who had played rugby for his country. Sergeant Jenkins would put Fishguard in the cells until he sobered up. We suspected he roughed him up often, for he would always keep very quiet for a few days afterwards. Now it was all agreed with the gang that if ever anything did happen to Pryce, they would have a whip-round for his family, but not one, for all had taken an oath, would attend his funeral. We all knew the local clergy would not bury him, for all knew of his evil reputation.

One day Sergeant Jenkins came into the bar and told us that Fishguard Pryce had finally met his end. It was in a dockside brawl in Liverpool and he had finished up in the Mersey, but his body had been recovered and brought home.

A collection was made for the family and gifts of food and comforts for the boys were taken to the house by Sergeant Jenkins.

There was only one subject of discussion over the next few days. Who would bury the old reprobate? Our vow not to attend still stood, and when Sergeant Jenkins came into the bar and put the time and date of the funeral on the darts board all surged forward to see who would officiate. Sergeant Jenkins stood back smiling. 'I have got a preacher for him,' he said, 'and one who will say something good over the body.'

This we had to hear because who could say anything at all nice for Fishguard Pryce? It was a Salvation Army captain, a recent newcomer to our midst, but the Army always looked after the sinners. The graveside was crowded with the village and all the regulars. The captain spoke and there was dead silence.

'Before the committal I would like to say a few words about the departed.' A whisper ran through the throng: now for it.

'Brethren, we are here to bury Fishguard Pryce, whose real name was William Daniel Pryce.' The murmur ran through the crowd again.

'Brethren,' said the captain, 'one thing I can say, our friend William Daniel Pryce was a good whistler.'

Richard Murdoch
Actor

It is interesting to speculate that if and when a Channel tunnel is completed, the RNLI on the south coast should have many fewer ships in distress to rescue. When the tunnel company put out tenders for the work most of the really big firms put in their bids amounting to many millions. The company was intrigued, however, by a tender from a Mr Alfred Perkins of Rotherhithe for £785 18s 4d. They asked Mr Perkins to be interviewed and he was asked how he could undertake the work for such a reasonable sum.

'Ah, well!' said Mr Perkins. 'My brother Charlie and I have two sets of equipment. He would start digging from Calais and I would start from Dover and we would meet in the middle.'

When asked what would happen if they miscalculated and didn't meet, he replied, 'Oh, then you'd get two tunnels for the price of one.'

Commander Brian Miles
Deputy Director, RNLI

The Aberdeen Lifeboat Ball is one of the city's major social functions and the lifeboat crew, always invited as guests of honour, swap their oilskins for full evening wear. One year the inevitable happened – there was a lifeboat call in the middle of the ball. The crew rushed off and launched the lifeboat. The job was to take a man with appendicitis off a ship and as it was a relatively easy task and a calm night, the coxswain did not insist on the men dressing in their oilskins, but simply ordered them to put on their lifejackets. The rendezvous with the ship was made, and as the lifeboat came alongside, the ship's skipper leaned over the side to see the lifeboat crew all immaculately dressed in dinner jackets. 'I knew you blokes give a good service,' he said, 'but this is bloody ridiculous!'

David Buckworth
Coxswain, Redcar Lifeboat

It was a warm sunny May afternoon, with a light breeze blowing and right on top of high water. As I looked out to sea I could not believe my eyes. A 1500-ton coaster was steaming straight towards the shore. The coastguard fired a warning maroon but it was too late. The ship struck the Saltscar rocks about a mile north east of the lifeboat station, putting a split in her about thirty feet long. Within minutes Redcar lifeboat was launched and we were soon alongside the stricken ship *Hen-*

drika. She was going down by the head and starting to list to starboard. Over the starboard side we could see a liferaft with a coloured seaman inside; I am sure to this day that he was beginning to turn white with fear.

We quickly rigged a tow, the idea being to try and refloat the ship and then to beach her again on the sand. The Tees pilot cutter came on scene and also rigged a tow. Shortly afterwards, Cullercoats Radio relayed a message: 'From master, *Hendrika* – stop pulling my ship. She is sinking.'

We slipped the tow and quickly came about and up on to the ship's port side to take off four crewmen, the master's wife and the master's son, a small lad of about eight or nine. The master and engineer stayed on board.

As we came round the ship, sounding the depth, it seemed as though the lifeboat was developing engine trouble. Each engine faltered and it looked like one or both might cut out. There was no obvious explanation, until we saw the young lad, totally unconcerned about his father and his ship, running round the lifeboat pushing and pulling all the knobs he could find. He had pulled out our engine stops!

To try and distract him, I gave him a German lifeboat coin which I kept in my pocket and this kept him quiet for a while. His mother explained to her son what the coin was and this helped to take her mind off what was going on around her. Our inflatable lifeboat came to ferry the survivors ashore, but the boy refused to return my coin, so I had to buy it back from him for ten pence.

We stood by the *Hendrika* for a short while but soon the master started to blow the fog horn. The list to starboard was getting worse. We steamed under the ship's bottom, which was now starting to show, and the master and engineer slid down the ship's side into our waiting lifeboat.

Meanwhile on shore, the lad was continuing to cause havoc. My ten pence had been spent on a large ice cream and, full of life and talk, the boy had to explore everything, using his tired mother as a translator. When we got back, he told us he had enjoyed a great day and asked, 'Will everybody be coming back again tomorrow so we can do it again?'

Postscript
The *Hendrika* came off the rocks on the next morning tide and sank. She was written off, a salvage attempt failed and she was later blown up. Each year we receive a Christmas card from the master inscribed, 'To our friends at Redcar'.

Paul Heiney
Television reporter

The lifeboat was called out by VHF to a yacht in trouble in dirty weather. The rescuers were trying to get the yacht's exact location; the coastguard called it on the radio.

'What is your position? Repeat, what is your position?'

And the answer came, faint but determined, from the skipper.

'My position . . . well, I am the marketing director of a medium-sized computer software firm in the east Midlands . . .'

P. Denham Christie

Former Chairman, RNLI Boat Committee;
former Coxswain, Tynemouth Lifeboat

More years ago than I care to remember, when I was coxswain of Tynemouth lifeboat, we received late one night a call to a trawler. She was on her way from the fishing grounds home to the Humber. Her chief engineer had fallen into her main engine and damaged himself. She would be four miles off the Tyne at one in the morning; would we meet her and take the engineer to hospital?

We launched at midnight and were a couple of miles off the river when we received a message. The engines of the trawler, having disposed of the chief engineer, were playing up, and the second engineer could only coax half-revolutions out of them. She would therefore be about an hour late at the rendezvous.

We were wondering what to do to keep ourselves busy while we waited, when we spied a huge dark shape at anchor a mile or so away. This was the largest tanker ever built in Britain to date, now on sea trials and waiting for daylight. We went close alongside, called her on our loudhailer, and asked if she was the fishing boat which was in trouble. We had evidently pricked the bubble of her pride, for the string of abuse we received in reply was judged by the experts amongst our crew to be masterly.

We had been considering going aboard and sharing her watch keeper's sandwiches, but came to the conclusion, after what had been said, that this might be unwise. However, while we were debating what to do next, the coastguard called us by lamp. The trawler would be even later; would we come in for an hour or so as a meal had been laid on for us?

Would we come in for a meal? Of course we would! So a couple of hours later, replete with soup and sandwiches, we climbed down into the boat and cast off to meet the trawler, who had reported herself to be some eight miles off the river.

As we moved off, someone threw into the boat a very early copy of the morning paper. We opened it, and there, to our great surprise and joy, right in the middle of the front page, was a glowing account of the service which we had yet to perform!

Janet Fookes
Member of Parliament

A few years ago I was approached by a woman's magazine asking if I would participate in their 'Day in the Life of . . .' series. They wanted to spend a day with me in my constituency to see what kind of activities I undertook. I agreed and a particular Friday was settled upon, though I pointed out that it was my custom to go by the midnight sleeper from Paddington to Plymouth on the Thursday night/Friday morning, and to be authentic they ought to accompany me. However the reporter and the photographer 'chickened out' of this, spending the night at a hotel in Plymouth and meeting me from the station at eight o'clock in the morning.

I had a very busy schedule that day, including a visit to the lifeboat station at Plymouth. Unexpectedly, while on the visit I was asked if I would care to have a ride in the lifeboat. I gleefully accepted and donned the brightly coloured orange waterproof gear that I was offered. Once the lifeboat was safely out into Plymouth Sound I was asked if I would like to take the wheel for a short while. I accepted with alacrity, always being willing to try anything once! I found this experience exhilarating, especially when I found confidence to put on speed and we whipped across the Sound, which was quite choppy, in dashing style. My day was made, as they say, when I learned quite by accident that the unfortunate reporter and photographer accompanying me were being discreetly sick. It made up, I thought, for all the times I had been misreported by the press!

Pat Dyas
Chairman, Royal Yachting Association

I joined a Yeomanry Regiment in 1940 as a very young officer. There were months of tough training in England before our armoured brigade embarked in August 1941 (tanks and all) and set off for the Middle East. Eventually, we became part of the 7th Armoured Division (the so-called Desert Rats), and got to know Tobruk, Benghazi and the desert very well. One day I was slightly wounded (enough to be sent back to Cairo), and then in hospital I contracted some form of rheumatic fever. As El Alamein was approaching, the hospital authorities were evacuating all those who couldn't walk. Before one realized what was happening it was hospital train, hospital ship and, in three weeks, Durban, and up to Johannesburg. The South African medical teams were superb, and in three months, after a final medical check-up, I was to be sent back to UK.

I boarded a troopship in Durban – the *SS Orcades*, already carrying elderly families leaving India, a group of nuns and some bomb-happy soldiers. First stop Cape Town to refuel, a few happy days meeting old friends, then out to sea again, unescorted. Twenty-four hours later we were in the Cape rollers, and blowing about force five. At midday, I got myself a pink gin, and was reading Oscar Wilde, when there was a sudden thump! A signal blew for 'surface attack', requiring passengers to go below. In my cabin I grabbed a lifejacket, a sheepskin coat and a flask of rum. Four more large bangs and the call for boat stations was sounded, and everyone assembled on deck. We had been torpedoed by the first of the long-range submarines to get down south.

SS Orcades was rolling strongly, and launching the lifeboats needed patience. It was only at the third attempt (the falls having jammed twice) that our ship's lifeboat, fully loaded with about eighty people, including civilians and a few nuns, hit the water. We started rowing, truly just keeping the bow into the waves, and into one's mind came the question, 'How far from shore?' – and the answer was, probably around three hundred miles.

I found myself rowing beside a sergeant major from one of the Royal tank regiments. After a bit, as we pulled the same oar, he looked across and saw my regimental badges.

'Oh, sir,' he said, 'you must know Captain Rosekilly.'

'Yes, he's a very good friend,' I replied.

'Oh, sir, when you next see him, do give him my regards!'

Dave Kennett
Coxswain, Yarmouth Lifeboat

One very rough night in the English Channel a yacht put out a distress message. She was about twenty-five miles south of our station. The Viking car ferry went to her position and stood by until we arrived in the lifeboat.

Conditions were appalling as we escorted this boat through the night and into the early hours of the morning. The yacht's crew must have felt very relieved when we eventually reached the relative calm and safety of the Solent and passed the Needles. Obviously they relaxed a bit too much after their long ordeal, because as we led them up the Channel the yacht went smack bang into the middle of the Sconce Buoy. It just goes to show that until you get in the harbour you're not safe.

*   *   *

We are a very busy lifeboat station with around fifty calls a year and we train every Sunday morning, so I have a first-class, experienced crew. Usually on rescues everything goes well but once, when we had to put on a demonstration for the RNLI's medical and survival committee, everything seemed to go wrong.

It was a very fine day with perfect weather and a slight breeze. We duly picked up about twelve very professional people – surgeons and doctors in the top of their league – and we proceeded down towards Hurst Castle. The idea was that one of our lads would jump over the side and be picked up either by the lifeboat or by the rubber boat we carry. In the event we decided to use the rubber boat because it's the most suitable thing to get a person out of the water before transferring to the lifeboat. The assistant mechanic agreed to jump over the side. The rubber boat was immediately launched at great speed, to impress these doctors, and two lifeboatmen jumped in to proceed to the casualty.

The first thing that happened was that one of the chaps jumped on to the fuel lead to the outboard motor, pulling off the fitting, and after two or three seconds the engine stopped. In the meantime our casualty for the exercise swam ashore. We then rescued the rubber boat.

We still carried on with the exercise. One of the items the committee wanted to look at was the resuscitation equipment we used, as it was a unique arrangement of oxygen bottles which had been a gift from local people. The committee asked the lifeboat inspector to demonstrate that we could use this equipment properly. He assured them that we had a very good crew on board. He said to me, 'Look, Dave, make sure you pick the right chap for this exercise because it's got to be right.' We had one ex-navy man on board, who acted as the casualty and pretended to collapse in the cabin. A crew member, who we assumed would be fully conversant with the gear, his wife being a nurse, rushed to his assistance and put the mouthpiece in. The casualty was soon gasping for breath because no one had remembered to turn on the oxygen set. When the patient started to go blue the oxygen was turned on and he was blown up until he was highly inflated. This didn't go down too well and the inspector was now tearing his hair out.

The next demonstration was to rendezvous with the Lymington lifeboat, which is an Atlantic 21, about half the length of our Arun class lifeboat. The Lymington crew were showing how their boat handled at speed and the helmsman was keeping his boat near our bow. He suddenly hit an awkward wave and the boat lost way under our bow. We struck it a glancing blow, taking with us the blue flashing light and radio aerial mounted on the stern of the Atlantic 21.

By this time the inspector obviously wished he was no longer a part of the exercise.

We then went to the Needles lighthouse to carry out a breeches buoy exercise. The ex-naval man in our crew was picked to fire the line, as he was experienced in this task. Again, we have often used the rocket line in rescues and have always been spot on target. This time, of course, the line completely missed and ended up right over the top of the

Needles Rock. The rubber boat was launched to recover the line but the repair we had made to the fuel pipe did not hold, the engine faded and the crew had to row to the Needles Rock, pick up the line and row across to the lighthouse.

It was a disastrous day. The inspector said to me, 'I think they need an inspector and a coxswain up in the Orkneys. Perhaps we ought to apply.'

George Mobbs
Former Coxswain, Gorleston Lifeboat

The night of 27 November 1954 saw the biggest shambles I have ever witnessed in the bend of Gorleston harbour in a gale of wind. Gorleston lifeboat received a message from the coastguards that there were five Polish drifters at the back of Gorleston pier and 'we cannot make out what they want'. It was blowing a severe sou'westerly gale and the coastguards asked us to launch the lifeboat to investigate.

We set out through a heavy sea over the harbour bar and made for the first drifter where we hailed the skipper to ask if he spoke English. 'Nein,' he replied in German. We went to the second drifter and asked the same question and again the answer was 'Nein'. The third drifter brought a third 'Nein'. Our coxswain, Bert Beavers, said, 'Well this is a rum job. We'll try the fourth one,' but we got the same reply.

At this point I happened to look over the stern of the lifeboat and I said to Bert, 'Them three are following us, they want us to pilot them into the harbour.' We took a round turn and the five drifters formed up in line astern of us. We had finally found out what they wanted.

While on passage to the harbour, the coastguards radioed that the wind was now reaching over 70 m.p.h. We entered the harbour and got the first four boats round the bend in the river, then the coxswain said, 'We'd better go back to see if the fifth one has crossed the bar OK.' But as we turned back, the four drifters all turned to follow us out again!

They could not understand what we tried to tell them to do. We led them to Freshing wharf, pointed to the quay and they tied up there. The coastguard then told us that the fifth boat had anchored off Britannia pier. We found a Dutch coaster captain who spoke German, went back to the first drifter and were thanked very much for all our help.

W.H. Osborne
Managing Director, William Osborne Ltd, Boatbuilders

The first launch of a new lifeboat from the builder's yard is usually a quiet occasion as the public ceremony takes place later at the lifeboat station with crowds, distinguished guests and, of course, the ritual smashing of a bottle of champagne over the bows. One of the lifeboats built by William Osborne Ltd attracted an unexpected but welcome crowd of visitors to witness the first launch, which was scheduled for 3 p.m. Someone had even told the press. Many of the shipyard staff stood admiring their handiwork as the lifeboat stood, on a trailer, at the top of the launching site. In spite of numerous successful launchings over the previous sixty-five years, this one did not go to plan. Well before three o'clock the lifeboat decided to launch herself along with the trailer and a member of the launching team.

When the reporters and photographers turned up they were surprised and disappointed to find no lifeboat at hand. Works director Reg Chatfield was asked for an explanation. With a wry smile he replied that she seemed very anxious to get in and it was now pointless hauling her out and starting all over again. A reporter remarked that at her official naming ceremony somebody would have to be pretty quick with the champagne if the lifeboat was going to behave so badly.

* * *

Every new self-righting lifeboat is tested by a simulated capsize and the Oakley class boat built by William Osborne Ltd for the station at Sheringham in Norfolk was no exception. However, Lord Saltoun, a member of the RNLI's committee of management and then seventy-five years old, was to witness the tests and asked that we lash him to the helm in the open cockpit for the final capsize. This was immediately ruled out, but we asked him why he wanted to do such a thing. He explained that he was a bad sailor and was always seasick, much to his embarrassment when he was at sea with a lifeboat crew. If we let him take part in the test, he could tell crews that he had been capsized in a lifeboat, upside down and back again, which they had not, and he prayed they never would.

Having listened to his lament, it was agreed that we could strap him down on a mattress in the engine room, and he was duly locked in behind the watertight door. The lifeboat was parbuckled by a heavy crane to an upside-down position. As she went over, the engines cut out as designed, a safety feature to avoid the propellers slashing anyone hanging on to the safety lines and to prevent the lifeboat setting off when she righted. Then a sudden, freak gust of wind entangled the lanyard that releases the sliphook around the main haul. The

67

lifeboat lay upside down for a whole minute instead of righting in five seconds. When she eventually came up, our men rushed aboard, unlocked the watertight door and untied his lordship. He emerged smiling and unscathed by his ordeal except for his trousers which were soaked in oil spilled from the engines while upside down. The drama ended with a bedraggled Lord Saltoun cheerfully suffering the indignity of standing in his underpants until a spare pair of trousers was found. He was anxious that his wife should not hear of the incident and a bond of secrecy was made. The next day's newspapers, with reports and photographs of Lord Saltoun's distress, showed that our bond was not quite watertight!

Norman Quillin
Coxswain, Port St Mary Lifeboat

Recent years have seen many inventions to improve the lot of the seafarer, but the most dramatic improvements must surely have been in communications, so that now, in an era of almost universal two-way radio, it becomes difficult to imagine the frustrations and mistakes of visual signalling methods of the not-too-distant past.

Radio has been a godsend not only to ships, but also to remote lighthouses. Nearly all of these were built in the nineteenth century, long before the days of radio communication, and were therefore fitted with yardarms on either side on which a series of black balls could be hung to convey basic messages to a distant shore observer.

My own experience of this system, when a lightkeeper on Lismore was laid low with appendicitis, did not fill me with confidence and must have filled the unfortunate patient with considerable apprehension. The appropriate permutation of black balls evoked no response from Oban for days on end, due to the prevalence of Scotch mist in that part of the world.

Years later, when a well-known character in the Northern Lighthouse service, Charlie Roberts, was principal keeper at the Chicken Rock lighthouse off the south-western corner of the Isle of Man, I recounted this episode during our return voyage to Port St Mary having just made a relief trip to the lighthouse. (I felt obliged to make conversation to deter him from giving the crew of the relief boat another rendering of 'Annie Laurie' on the one-string fiddle he had built during his last stint on the lighthouse.)

Charlie too had had his communications problems, it appeared, when he was on Pentland Skerries lighthouse. Once again the problem was a keeper with appendicitis, and the weather was far too bad for a boat to take him off. A system was arranged whereby the patient's pulse rate and temperature would be transmitted by Aldis lamp every evening, and a doctor on shore would interpret these and return instructions by the same means.

This worked well for two evenings, but on the third evening the watch had changed and a different lightkeeper was manning the Aldis. Symptoms were duly transmitted, and after a pause the reply winked back over the stormy waters of the Pentland Firth: 'Give treatment of two nights ago.'

Unfortunately our man on the Aldis found the Achilles heel of Samuel Morse's celebrated code and read this as: 'Give treatment of two night sago.'

The happy outcome of the tale was that the patient responded well to a diet of nocturnal milk puddings, and was on his feet by the time the storm abated and the relief boat came alongside. The good doctor, for his part, received a letter from the commissioners of Northern Lights thanking him for his devotion to duty and commending him for the efficacious treatment he had prescribed.

Derek Scott
Coxswain, Mumbles Lifeboat

Some years ago during one hot summer's night, around three in the morning, the coastguard at Mumbles Head received a message from a Norwegian tanker, which was at anchor, saying that a member of their crew had fallen overboard, and they requested a lifeboat immediately. The maroons were fired and I was on my way pedalling my bike to the boathouse.

Coming towards me in the dark, I saw a young man falling all over the road, obviously drunk. I tried to avoid him, but we collided. Explaining who I was, and the urgency of my mission, I managed to get rid of him and went on my way.

Minutes later, as I stood on the deck of the lifeboat with my crew, dressed and ready to go down the slipway, the drunk appeared, and started to climb the boarding ladder. Now, I am well used to what I call 'after-ten volunteers' (everyone wants to be a lifeboatman after the pub shuts), so I said to the biggest crew man, 'Get him off.'

While our unwanted guest was quite definitely being removed by his collar, he suddenly spun around and shouted, 'Stop! Don't launch that boat, I'm the one you are going to save.'

I was so taken aback by this statement that I jumped off the boat to hear what he had to say. It appeared that he, with a number of friends, had been celebrating. He was to be married the following day. After leaving the club at closing time they had decided to round off the proceedings with a moonlight cruise of the Bristol Channel, in a motor cruiser borrowed for the occasion.

During the voyage the young man went to the stern of the boat, unobserved by his friends, and jumped into a dinghy which was being towed behind and which contained a crate of beer. The tow-rope broke and the cruiser went off into the night leaving one passenger behind.

Some time later the party noticed that one of their number was missing and, unable to find him, headed for a nearby Norwegian tanker to raise the alarm. After boarding with some difficulty, they managed to reach the wireless operator who only had a smattering of English. He subsequently sent a message to the coastguard saying, 'One of my crew has fallen overboard,' and a lifeboat was requested.

In the meantime our hero, finding himself miles from the shore, in a dinghy, with a crate of beer, and on his own, started rowing like mad for home, and finally made it. But not before consuming that crate of beer. After all, it was a hot night.

Postscript
I did admire the way he told all those lifeboatmen, 'You can all go back to bed now, it was only me.' And he did get married that day.

Tony Purnell
Press Officer, West Mersea Branch, RNLI

Terry is a good crew member of our Atlantic 21 class lifeboat *Alexander Duckham*. About twelve months ago he discovered an added talent for photography, and became so good at it in a short space of time that we designated him 'unofficial station photographer' (local, acting and unpaid)! Many of his photographs in colour were put in a special album which was carefully kept up to date. This could be seen in the lifeboathouse and created great interest among visitors to the station, as well as being a record for posterity. In fact the quality was so good that when there was an event of note, Terry was asked to be handy in case the press bloke didn't turn up! Then, being a generous sort of guy, he decided to buy, at his own expense, a small camera for the lifeboat which could be stowed away unobtrusively.

Came a lifeboat exercise one Sunday in August. One of those quiet days, virtually 'harry flatters', the Blackwater estuary full of little boats and the possibility of a pint or two when our heroes returned!

Out by one of the large laid-up freighters moored in the estuary, it was suggested by John, another crew member, that it would be a 'good thing' to take a photo of various crew activities. Terry agrees – excellent idea.

John then questions, 'Is the camera waterproof?'

Says Terry proudly, 'My dear John, not only is it waterproof, but it is knockproof, bashproof and even crewproof. Look,' says he, and throws the camera over the side just to prove it.

Whereupon, under the fascinated gaze of John and the three other crew members, it gracefully sinks in thirty metres of water. Waterproof, yes; floatable, definitely not. Hilarious collapse of crew, and a rueful Terry decides that the next lifeboat camera shall have its own buoyancy aid!

Richard F. Barclay

RNLI Committee of Management

In the Row Hedge repair yard was a small lifeboat, which I think came from Eastbourne, which had been very badly shot up. The story I was told was that in 1940 certain lifeboats were selected to go to Dunkirk and the lifeboatmen took them to Dover, where they were disappointed to be relieved by naval crews for the Channel crossing. This boat worked on the beach at Dunkirk where it was strafed and quite severely damaged, with the result that it lay low in the water. The naval crew, who did not appreciate the characteristics of the lifeboat, abandoned her. She was carried by the current down the Dover straits and was observed by a French torpedo boat (in those days considerably heavier than the MTBs we saw later in the war). She regarded the lifeboat as a dangerous wreck and shelled her with a view to her sinking, but this had no result. She therefore decided to ram, but such was the toughness of the lifeboat's construction that the hole the torpedo boat made was not much bigger than the diameter of a bucket. According to the story, the torpedo boat sufficiently damaged its own bows to have to return to harbour. A day or two later the lifeboat was spotted, black with oil, off Newhaven. She was towed in and eventually was repaired and returned to station.

Colonel G.A. Jackson

Honorary Treasurer, Angle Branch, RNLI

It was a lovely summer's day,
In fact the last bank holiday.
The village pub was all ding dong –
The second cox'n in full song
(Smart yachtsmen from away
Were being allowed to pay).
The cox'n with a thoughtful frown
Sat behind a small Manns brown.

The landlord, in 'Time, please' tone
Said, 'Cox, you're wanted on the phone.'
I wonder now what is the matter
It could well be that damned regatta,
But no – it was Coastguard Jo
Spelling out a tale of woe –
Some foreign yacht had lost its mast
And was holed and sinking fast –
Please launch with all speed,
Their skipper really is in need.

Suddenly the quiet of the afternoon
Is shattered by the first maroon.

Quickly did the crew disperse
With many a gulp and curse.
Along the path they jog and stumble,
Mouthing oath and grumble,
On the slip a breathless hustle
As on board they barge and bustle.

Hurry on you lazy lags –
Oh hell, I've lost my fags –
Come give us now a hand to swing . . .
Don't forget, give Jo a ring . . .
The winchman slams the lever in,
The boat clanks out against the din.
It all looks totally confused
But down the years they've proved
Whenever there comes a need
That they can launch with speed.

All ready now, knock out that pin.
She's free and now starts sliding in.
Then with a great smack of spray
She is speeding on her way.

Edward Wake-Walker
Assistant Public Relations Officer, RNLI

A crowd of people on a busy beach had gathered around the inflatable lifeboat which had just come ashore. A small boy had drifted out in a rubber dinghy and, on the point of utter despair, had been found by the lifeboatmen and brought safely back to the beach. A large lady, pushing her way through the crowd, panted up to the lifeboat helmsman and asked, 'Are you the man who has just brought my little boy in?'

The helmsman, staring shyly at his boots, replied, 'You could say that, ma'am.'

'Well where's his hat, then?' was the astonishing demand.

Navy Blues

Bridge rôles and officers' mess

Dr Denis Rebbeck
Former Chairman, Harland and Wolff, Shipbuilders

Statement from Admiralty to our shipyard regarding the storage of torpedoes: 'It is necessary, for technical reasons, that these warheads should be stored with the top at the bottom and the bottom at the top and in order that there may be no doubt as to which is the bottom and which is the top, for storage purposes, it will be seen that the bottom of each head has been clearly marked with the word top.'

Sir Alec Guinness
Actor

In the spring of 1943 I was in command of one of the brand-new LCI(L)s which crossed the Atlantic, as a squadron, to North Africa, prior to the invasion of Sicily.

In Norfolk, Virginia, we were encouraged to camouflage our ships with paint in any style we fancied. I devised a pattern of pale blue and white rectangles, rather like a Braque painting. My fellow officers complained that I had made mine look like a hospital-ship and far too conspicuous; but when we were out on the ocean they equally complained that they couldn't see me. If they really couldn't see me some mornings, it was largely the fault of the steering-gear, which was electrical and had a nasty habit of seizing up, so that for hours, on two nights running, I found myself doing small circles in the middle of the Atlantic.

In command of the squadron was a delightful RN lieutenant commander who had a gentle, dry wit and was a dab hand at sending Biblical signals. On the morning after one of my individual night manoeuvres, as soon as I was recognized on the horizon as a pale blue smudge, he flashed his Aldis lamp, in morse code, 'Hebrews, Chapter 13, Verse 8.'

A watchkeeper was sent immediately to fetch a Bible. It was a lovely sunny morning and the breeze tugged exasperatingly at the India paper pages until I found the right place and got the signal: 'Jesus Christ, the same yesterday, today and for ever.'

Admiral of the Fleet
Sir Henry Leach
Former First Sea Lord

It was the opening day of the Atlantic-Channel Symposium, held at the Royal Naval College Greenwich under the joint sponsorship of Admiral Sir John Frewen (whose brainchild it was) and Admiral Eph Holmes USN, the two major NATO commanders concerned. I was Admiral Frewen's personal staff officer.

That first morning had gone well. Prince Philip had been present throughout, SACEUR (General Lemnitzer) had delivered a good address and CINCHAN (Admiral Frewen) had given an impressive *tour d'horizon* with punch and without notes. In it he had said some straight things about the French and their withdrawal from the integrated military structure of the Alliance. The French had not liked it and their three-man delegation had walked out of the conference hall.

At lunch the Painted Hall was filled to overflowing; a generous menu had been provided and ample time allowed for conversation and continuing discussion. The French did not attend but during the main course I learned that their delegation was waiting outside, determined to 'get' Admiral Frewen before he left. Clearly he should be warned of this and I scribbled a cryptic note to the effect on the back of a menu card. Summoning one of the Pensioner waiters to deliver it, I pointed out Admiral Frewen (whom he did not know) sitting at the high table next to Prince Philip (whom he did). He went off but returned seconds later having lost his nerve.

The brief was repeated in more explicit detail: 'The man with lots of gold braid on his sleeve, with black hair – next to Prince Philip in plain clothes, with fair hair.' Off he went again. I watched him carefully; surely this time it would work. He stumped off resolutely enough, mounted the steps to the upper hall, unhesitatingly went to the centre of the high table, and handed it to . . . a surprised Prince Philip.

Sometimes you can't win.

*   *   *

In the spring of 1949 the 2nd Minesweeping Flotilla, then engaged in operational mine clearance in the Mediterranean, paid an informal visit to Izmir (née Smyrna) in Turkey. As is customary in these parts, the ships were berthed stern to the jetty with two anchors down, and to get ashore involved more or less 'walking the plank' over some of the minesweeping gear before reaching the normal gangway; not difficult, but a manoeuvre which called for care and attention rather than panache.

On the day after our arrival Captain Keith Walter (commanding the flotilla) gave a lunch party in his cabin on board the leader, *HMS Fierce*. He was a big, well-built man whose almost outrageous good looks were a source of embarrassment and envy to the staff and junior officers less well endowed when it came to impressing the girls. The lunch party was an exclusive little affair *à deux*; Mrs Carruthers, the wife of an English magnate residing in the town, was also a strikingly handsome woman in her late thirties and had evidently caught the captain's eye at the previous evening's reception. She arrived punctually in a chauffeur-driven Rolls-Royce, negotiated the gangway with aplomb and presented her magnificent mink-clad figure to her host with a smile to capture kings. I was the duty officer.

At about 3.30 there were signs that the party was breaking up: was Mrs Carruthers's car alongside, etc? Though a glorious sunny day, there was a sharp nip in the air and the gangway staff were wearing watchcoats. No breath of wind stirred the glutinous slurry which formed the surface of the water in that part of the harbour, a mixture of waste fuel-oil, garbage and the usual flotsam and jetsam including several dead rats and a sheep; the crispness of the air acted as only a partial curb on the resultant aroma. The captain led his guest aft, deep in continuing conversation. It had been a convivial interlude and Mrs Carruthers had clearly been charmed by naval hospitality, to say nothing of the cultured *savoir faire* of her host. But now, alas, it was over.

'Goodbye, Captain Walter,' she said with a radiant smile and, gathering her voluminous fur coat about her ample frame, waving graciously with her disengaged hand, and continuing to murmur, 'Thank you, thank you *so* much, a really lovely party . . .' she mounted backwards the three steps leading to 'the plank' and, with a final genial flourish, disappeared straight over the side to join the rats and the sheep in the oily mush of Izmir inner harbour.

Reaction on board was swift. Without hesitation Able Seaman Brown, the quartermaster, stripped off his heavy watchcoat and leaped over the side to the rescue. The rest of us then witnessed the paradox of the century. For Able Seaman Brown, though brave and loyal and gallant to a fault, was quite unable to swim. On the other hand Mrs Carruthers was an exceedingly good swimmer and, grasping the hapless quartermaster in the approved manner, she ably towed him through the oil and muckage to the jetty steps and so to survival. There, having mounted the steps herself and with filthy black water streaming off her, she turned to the ship with a last triumphant wave and got into her Rolls past the horrified gaze of her chauffeur. The rich squelch as she sank contentedly back into the ivory-coloured upholstery was unforgettable.

And Able Seaman Brown? Well, what do you think?

Ursula Stuart Mason
Public Relations Officer, National Maritime Museum

Saint Peter was checking in the new arrivals at the Heavenly Gate, when an admiral and his lady appeared together.

'Good gracious,' said Saint Peter, 'whatever makes you think I'm going to let you in here?' The couple looked rather discomfited. 'You', said Saint Peter to the admiral, 'have allowed your whole life to be dominated by drink. Even your wife is called Ginny. No, you can't come in – go away and find somewhere else.'

Hard on their heels came another pair – this time a captain and his wife. Saint Peter looked at his checklist.

'You can't come in,' he said to the captain. 'Your whole life has been dominated by money. Even your wife is called Penny. Go away and find somewhere else.'

They too turned sadly away. The next couple in line, a commander and his wife, had heard something of both conversations and before they faced Saint Peter the commander turned to his wife and said, 'Come on, Fanny, I'm not staying here to be insulted.'

Robin Knox-Johnston
Round-the-world Yachtsman

In 1968, when I was a watchkeeping officer in one of Her Majesty's frigates, I was on duty when we carried out a live firing exercise with our anti-submarine mortars. To do this we had to find a deserted area of sea, because if a fishing boat was even a smudge on the horizon, the owner would put in claim of damaged something to the Admiralty the moment he heard

the explosions. The effect of salvoes of mortar bombs is pretty terrific and it was usual for us to arrange to have a bit of time free afterwards, so that we could pick up the fish that were stunned or killed by the explosions. This provided a welcome change to our diet.

After about ten minutes, we lowered our two boats, steamed slowly into the area, and started to pick up a very satisfactory number of large cod. I was leaning over the bridge and watching the attempts of three or four seamen to catch one particularly large fish with a grapnel, but they were not having much success and it was obvious that we would soon drift past and lose the fish. At that moment there was a large splash from aft and a yell of 'Man overboard starboard side'. I ordered the engines to stop and started to recall our boats, when I observed the 'casualty', AB Booth, our ship's cook, spluttering to the surface about fifteen feet clear of the ship.

He was quickly recovered, but as we hauled him aboard we noticed a large fish-tail sticking out of the top of his shirt. He had jumped in to recover the large cod. Normally his behaviour would have been punished but I explained to the captain that it was an accident and the captain, who did not miss much, smilingly accepted my explanation.

We had fresh fish and chips for the entire ship's company for three days after that little haul!

Rear Admiral Morgan Giles
RNLI Committee of Management

At the Salerno landings in 1943, a young lieutenant RNVR, newly in command of a small landing craft, steamed from port to starboard straight across the bows of a battleship.

The captain sent a sarcastic signal: 'Have you a copy of the rule of the road on board?'

Immediate reply from the landing craft: 'Yes – what is it you wish to know?'

Lord Longford
Author

Nearly all my ancestors were military, but there were several admirals among them. I myself am the least maritime of men. In, however, what is called a typically British fashion, I served as First Lord of the Admiralty, a post, alas, now abolished, in the last few months of the Attlee government of 1945-51.

In that capacity, I visited Dartmouth and presided over the early morning prayers. Suddenly the order was given: 'Roman Catholics fall out!' I was a fairly recent convert to Catholicism (only eleven years' standing). Some subconscious sense of persecution overtook me. I stepped rapidly backwards, causing no small confusion among the high-ranking officers surrounding me. They were too polite and well-disciplined to refer to the incident afterwards. I plucked up courage to ask why most of the Catholics were coloured. It was explained to me that there were considerable attachments from the Egyptian, Pakistani and Iranian navies. 'Catholics' was a generic term applied to all 'lesser breeds' – though I am sure that expression was not used.

Rear Admiral D.W. Haslam
Hydrographer of the Navy

After the revolution in Zanzibar my ship, *HMS Owen*, had successfully arranged the safe custody and eventual evacuation of the British women and children to Mombasa before several major warships could get out to the scene. Eventually an aircraft carrier arrived with a very senior captain in command who sent a helicopter to collect me to brief him on the current situation. Being very much at the top end of the zone for promotion, I wanted to impress, so I donned a brand new pair of white tropical shorts. I had to be winched off my forecastle and, in those days, one did not have to wear protective air-clothing. The wire strop was lowered, put under my arms and I gave the thumbs-up sign to be hoisted aloft. As soon as the weight came off my feet, I took in a deep breath and my trousers fell down.

*   *   *

A young lieutenant commander, having taken his first command safely from his berth in North Yard, Devonport, and passed the Torpoint Ferry, was so relieved that he flashed up a cigarette on his bridge before passing Mount Wise.

Flag officer, Plymouth's telescope spotted this and the CO soon received a signal: 'Why were you smoking a cigarette when your hands were still fallen in for leaving harbour?'

'Because I don't smoke a pipe,' was quickly (and foolishly) signalled back.

During the day's sea-trials, the CO regretted his flippancy and, on repassing Mount Wise that evening he was spotted (by the admiral) with the binnacle cover over his head. To the signal, 'Why were you wearing a binnacle cover when entering harbour?' the reply was made, 'After this morning's effort, it will be the only brass hat that I shall ever wear.'

* * *

One weekend I went to stay with the parents of my seven-year-old godson and found I had to share a bedroom with him. Not wishing to wake him when I went up in the early hours, I crept into the room and took the pyjamas from under my pillow and went into the bathroom to change. To my surprise when I went back to the room, my godson had put on the light and was kneeling by his bed, with his back to me, saying his prayers. Thinking to do my godparental duty, I did likewise by my bed.

Immediately, my godson asked, 'What are you doing, Uncle David?'

Rather embarrassed, I replied, 'The same as you are.'

'Well you're going to make an awful mess 'cos there is no potty under your bed!'

Clive Hunting
Chairman, Hunting Group of Companies

It is a misty October night in the English Channel in 1943. British motor torpedo boats are on their way across the Channel to look for enemy coastal shipping or E boats moving under the cover of darkness. A British cruiser is making her way down-Channel when her radar shows up the small craft and the cruiser slows down. The mist lifts and searchlights soon show up the MTBs.

An Aldis lamp taps out the message to the leading boat: 'Consider yourself lucky, all my six-inch guns are pointing straight at you.'

Back comes the immediate answer: 'Consider yourself even luckier, I have just fired two torpedoes at you!'

Sir John Moore
Second Crown Estate Commissioner

Our half-flotilla of four destroyers was being put through some exercise manoeuvres at high speed, while on passage through the channel swept for mines down the east coast. Creaming along in line abreast, and thereby covering a half-mile strip of the North Sea, we came on a unit of small grey minesweepers, earnestly and devotedly about their never-ending and dangerous task of keeping the channel safe, for destroyers and convoys alike.

With traditional Royal Navy courtesy, the senior officer of

the destroyers signalled to the sweepers, 'Good afternoon. Thank you for your care in cultivating the manure heap.'

The leading minesweeper replied, 'We much appreciate your thanks, and the confidence shown by your broadminded approach to our problem.'

*　*　*

Harwich Harbour was quite used to the antics of the motor torpedo boats based at *HMS Beehive*, the Felixstowe dock. But surely one of the strangest performances must have been that of MTB 352 one summer afternoon in 1943. She came rushing out of the dock unusually fast, with sailors still tidying up the upper deck in most unprepared fashion. She did not head for the open sea but darted over to Shotley, about a mile away. And there she sat, for over an hour, doing nothing but manoeuvre fiercely so that no matter what the wind or tide did, she kept her square stern pointedly and obviously towards the dock whence she came.

The explanation was unusual. *Beehive* was a most enterprising place, and an impatient one. If we thought we needed more guns, we would 'rescue' those of a boat we had lost – and forget to mention it. Then we would scheme to mount this extra armament on another boat. Strictly, any such idea needed rigorous experiment, testing and authorization. We were in a hurry and did not wait. We did our own thing and learned our lessons as they happened. That was how MTB 352 came to have a powerful twin 20mm cannon on the foredeck, as well as the legitimate replica down aft. Useful – but quite unapproved by *HMS Excellent* (the Navy's gunnery establishment), and likely to cause great embarrassment if they found out. So when two of *Excellent*'s gunnery officers appeared unannounced at *Beehive*, something had to be done very quickly. My orders were simply: 'Get 352 out of the dock at once; and don't let anyone here see your foredeck until these blighters have gone.' It was an unusual sailing instruction – but it worked.

Donald Sinden
Actor

During 1952 I was involved in the filming of Nicholas Monsarrat's *The Cruel Sea*. For one scene I was in charge of the fo'c'sle gun which had to be fired in a scene shot at night. We were provided with regulation earplugs and anti-flash helmets. The camera and director were on the bridge looking down on us. I had to be looking ahead through binoculars and when I heard 'Action!' I was to say, 'Fire', the leading gunner would relay the order by saying 'Shoot', and off should go the four-inch gun. Everything seemed ready and we were considerably nervous. I had no previous experience of standing that close to a gun – and the gun had not been used for some years. 'ACTION!' He had to shout it twice before I could hear it through my earplugs: 'FIRE', 'SHOOT'. There followed a noise no louder than a fifth of November banger and out from the muzzle fell a wad of burning cotton wool! Obviously we would have to do it again and I thought I could assist communication if I removed my earplugs. Unbeknown to me the director decided to use a live round. As I awaited my cue I peered through my binoculars and spied a light on the horizon. Suddenly 'ACTION!' 'FIRE', 'SHOOT', and my eardrums were nearly ruptured as a live round whistled off. A flashing Aldis lamp in the distance informed us that we had missed a cargo ship by about a hundred feet! I felt that it would not assist matters if I admitted I had seen the other ship.

As a goodwill gesture some of the actors agreed to attend the WRNS tennis tournament. I found myself sitting next to the gym instructress, a tall, massive lady with short-cropped, iron-grey hair and a moustache. She was wearing 'plain clothes', a thick tweed suit, thick-knit stockings and heavy brogue shoes. She had a powerful contralto bark. Tea was to be taken in the wardroom and our way lay through the gymnasium. As we entered, she suddenly clouted me on the back and roared, 'Race you up a rope.' I have never felt more effeminate in my life.

On another occasion the publicity man came on the set and asked me to meet one of the senior officers of the WRNS, who was seated some distance behind the camera. In the comparative darkness I extended my hand and sat beside her. I thought I would tell her my gym instructress story. I got as far as 'short-cropped, iron-grey hair'; my eyes were getting used to the dim light and I saw that she too had short-cropped, iron-grey hair . . . I continued, 'She was wearing tweeds and thick-knit stockings . . .' To my horror I saw that she was dressed identically. But I could not stop now. I got to the tag line, 'Race you up a rope.' The officer turned to a companion whom I now noticed for the first time – she too was identical. The first slapped the second on the back and, roaring with laughter, cried, 'That must have been Basher Gibson!'

From *A Touch of the Memoirs* (Hodder & Stoughton)

Rear Admiral Desmond Hoare
Former Headmaster, Atlantic College

For two years during the war I was chief engineer of the battleship *King George V*. I got the job very young, by accident, and was naturally much in awe and admiration of our captain, Tom Halsey. He was the last naval officer to have taken leave of absence as a sub-lieutenant to sail, before the mast, to Australia in a full-rigged sailing ship. He was roughly the same shape as Winston Churchill and immensely strong. When in harbour he always came up to the wardroom for a gin before dinner. If an officer happened to be standing in the way as he entered he would be picked up under the arms and thrown to the nearest sofa. One day Tom picked up the fleet constructor officer but missed the sofa. The commander-in-chief, Admiral Tovey, was not pleased.

One evening just before Christmas Tom sent for me to tell me in great secrecy that we were leaving at 0800 tomorrow to fetch Winston Churchill home from Gibraltar. We all knew that Winston had been recuperating in Morocco from a serious illness. So we left Scapa at high speed. The Germans must not know about such a precious cargo so Tom had to bring the great battleship into the small harbour at Gibraltar after dark without lights. At about 2000 a familiar bulky figure came up the gangplank and was escorted by Tom back to the captain's aft cabin. We had about 3000 tons of oil to take on and I was told to report progress hourly. After the first hour I found the two of them drinking horse's necks, naval jargon for brandy and ginger ale, and Winston talking, talking, talking. After the second hour ditto, and so on to the eighth hour when I could say, 'Ready to go, sir.' Winston had to sleep in the safest place, judged to be forward just under the bridge. So the procession started, master at arms leading. All went well until the steel ladders which led up from the main deck to the bridge. Here Winston hit his forehead on a coaming and blood flowed. Never was the surgeon commander produced so fast, and Winston never stopped talking for one moment, to the fascination of the motley observers. Out of the harbour again without lights and 'full speed' was rung down to maintain thirty-one knots to Plymouth.

Winston was not an early riser but spent most of the day wandering round the ship talking to the crowds that gathered everywhere. Winston had to have his war map room and this meant he had to have his WRNS to stick the pins in.

The commander organized a dance in the wardroom, and as French chalk was not a war store, the cabins of some of the more sissy officers were raided for talcum powder. The mixture of smells for the first hour cannot be described. During the dance Winston sat on a sofa and talked. We took it in turns to sit with him and listen. I have never heard anything like it, so much history, wit and wisdom stored up behind the piece of sticking plaster.

Apart from a Junkers 88 scare in the Bay, mistaken of course, in naval fashion of those days, as 'one of ours', and sliding over a wreck in Cawsand bay, the cargo was safely delivered to the Great Western Railway.

Winston went on to glory. Tom, who would have made the best First Sea Lord since the war, contracted TB and was invalided into obscurity.

Rear Admiral Wilfred Graham
Director, RNLI

A new, young and very keen cadet at the Britannia Royal Naval College was paraded in front of the commander, charged with the grievous offence of smuggling on board intoxicating liquor.

The divisional officer presented the case for the prosecution, culminating with the production of the evidence which was a miniature bottle of some evil-smelling liqueur.

The commander invited the divisional officer to sample the evidence. This he did and said he considered that it was alcoholic. The commander then swigged down the rest and said he thought that it was pretty noxious.

Having done that, he turned to the cadet and said that as the evidence no longer existed there appeared to be no foundation for pursuing the charge any further. The cadet was duly admonished on the evils of liquor and of flouting regulations, and was then sent on his way rejoicing.

Leon Goossens
Oboist

A very young and striving midshipman was piloting a party of VIPs on a visit to the flagship in an admiral's pinnace. He was very much daunted at the sight of the welcoming party awaiting his arrival and this had the effect of diminishing his powers of seamanship, causing him to make a faulty approach and forcing him to turn away for another try. At his last attempt a stentorian voice on the loudhailer echoed the words, 'All right, sir, stay where you are, we'll come alongside you!'

*   *   *

During a concert tour in 1942 which included a visit to the Royal Navy in Scapa Flow, I was being ferried from the flagship *King George V* to my quarters on Flotta in a drifter. I was togged up in dinner suit and black tie on that occasion and, feeling rather hot, I stood leaning on the rail breathing in the fresh night air, when I was soon joined by a grimy young engineer smoking a pipe. He eyed me up and down, wondering how to approach me in conversation.

Eventually, clearing his throat, he said, 'What mob are you?' I was so surprised that I had to think hard before I answered but eventually I was able to say that I was one of a concert party having just entertained the ship's company with some music. He thought for a few seconds and then said, 'ENSA, I suppose.'

'Well, not exactly!' said I. 'We are known as CEMA.'

His final retort: 'Oh, I get you . . . amateurs.'

Vice Admiral Sir David Hallifax

Deputy Supreme Allied Commander Atlantic

I was appointed as a sub-lieutenant to my first ship – an Algerine-class minesweeper – in Malta. As Christmas approached, arrangements were made for the ship's company to enjoy the festive season on board in the traditional manner –

without carrying either festivity or tradition too far. It all worked pretty well. We invited the captain to Christmas lunch in the wardroom. This was such a success that the captain sent for the PO cook to congratulate him. He was a Maltese petty officer generally known by his Christian name of Hannibal; he was quite short, very round and always smiling. As he entered the wardroom wearing an apron but no shirt, it was evident that his smile was even broader than usual and that the Christmas spirit was already strong within him. He went round to each officer to shake him by the hand, sweating a good deal from his exertions in the galley. It wasn't until he turned to wobble his way happily out of the door that we all realized that he wasn't just wearing an apron and no shirt – it was an apron and nothing else. He retreated with careful dignity to his hot little galley, conscious of nothing other than a job well done – and after all, anybody can get absent-minded at Christmas.

* * *

I was serving in an aircraft carrier as a senior lieutenant under a wonderful captain whose talent for getting out of trouble was as great as his talent for getting into it. After passing through the Suez Canal we had had one or two collisions – the last one with a large disabled tanker which we were trying to take in tow. Her bow punched a hole in our stern, and although there was no structural damage the captain wanted a cosmetic repair completed before returning home through the canal. The shipwrights task-welded some plates over the hole, but had to leave a smaller hole for the last man to climb back inboard from the stage on which he had been working. The captain said the hole had to be filled in completely, so the air engineers constructed a vast brass cone over six feet long with spikes sticking out of the end, and with a coloured ball on the end of each spike. This was made to fill the remaining gap, and poked out of our stern looking rather unusual. As we went through the canal, the Egyptians could be seen frantically photographing this absurd device from every angle. As they were on 'the other side' at that time, we presumed that the photographs were sent to Moscow. To our great sadness, we never heard what the Soviet analysts made of them – but even if they had been told the truth, they certainly would not have believed it.

Admiral of the Fleet
The Lord Hill-Norton
Former First Sea Lord and Chief of Defence Staff

In the 1930s many of our cruisers, and some battleships too, carried a seaplane for reconnaissance and gunnery-spotting. The naval officer pilot and observer carried out the normal duties of a lieutenant onboard when not flying.

While at anchor in the Greek islands one fine day in 1937 the pilot, Lieutenant Trubshaw, was officer of the watch in his frock coat on the quarterdeck of *HMS Nonsuch*. The ship's motorboat returned from a duty trip to the shore and, in accordance with custom, the cox'n – a leather-faced, three-badge leading seaman – asked the officer of the watch for further orders.

'Make fast to the starboard yardarm, please,' said Trubshaw.

Saluting smartly, the cox'n sped off and tore round the ship at full speed, making no attempt to secure to the lower boom.

On his second circuit Trubshaw bellowed out, 'What the blankety-blank do you think you are doing?' to which the cox'n, saluting smartly again, replied, 'A couple more times round, sir, and I'll take off a treat.'

Commander R.D. Wall
Former Deputy Director, Maritime Trust

In the days of yore before the awful word 'communications' became current in service jargon, the conduct of the British fleet was governed to a large extent by signals and the Holy Bible. To the young naval officer sensible of what was good for him, these were to each other as angostura bitters is to gin and all four were assiduously imbibed. From the time of Nelson, and before, much transmission time has been saved by quoting chapter and verse of an apposite passage from the Bible.

As in the case of Commander G.H. Stokes, Royal Navy, when he was captain of the destroyer *Sikh*.

Now it came to pass in the year 1941 that this same Stokes was made commander over four destroyers and straightway charged by those in authority over him to convoy safely from Alexandria in Egypt to the island of Malta some merchant ships bearing ammunition for those who defended the island. And so sore was the need of the defenders for these things that the high officers at Alexandria charged Stokes that he proceed forthwith and with all speed, deviating neither to the left nor to the right, to seek out the enemy lest he be diverted from the chief task with which he was charged.

But it came to pass after several days that on drawing nigh unto Malta in the dark watch before the dawn there passed to the eastward two cruisers of the navy of the Italian enemy. And Stokes, having eyes like unto those of the night hawk, did see their passing. But the Italians saw him not and they, though being more powerful, were caught wanting in diligence and were even destroyed by the torpedoes of the smaller ships of Stokes. And Stokes and all his sailors went on their way rejoicing into Malta, but holding his peace for was there not the rule of radio silence in time of war.

And in their going, about the time of the dawn, there passed over them, with great noise towards the place they had just left, a squadron of naval aircraft. And the bellies of the aircraft were big with torpedoes. It was not vouchsafed to Stokes that the captain of all these aircraft also rejoiced in his heart for that he had been sent forth by the chief commander in Malta to destroy with the dawn the cruisers of the Italians and add lustre to his name thereby. But though he searched diligently he found not that which he had been charged to destroy. And his heart was heavy within him and his left breast felt naked for want of the blue and red ribbon which is given by the King as a sign to mark those who have been valiant in battle.

And it came to pass that when he and those under him, all having the taste of ashes in their mouths, returned to their camp in Malta, it was revealed to them what Stokes had done. And they were exceedingly wrathful and caused a signal to be sent to Stokes in his ship. And these were the words which the men of the aircraft sent to the men of the ships.

To SIKH
From CO 816 Squadron
Saint John Chapter Ten Verse One
AR.

For the benefit of the heathen, being not naval officers and therefore wanting in biblical knowledge, the passage referred to reads:

Verily, verily, I say unto you, He that entereth not by the door into the sheepfold but climbeth up some other way, the same is a thief and a robber.

Sir Julian Ridsdale
Member of Parliament

The night sleeper was fully booked. A pretty girl had to get home. She asked a sailor for his accommodation which he was persuaded into giving her.

He cabled, 'Sorry shall be late from leave, given berth to a girl.'

The commanding officer cabled back, 'Your next confinement will be to barracks!'

Ursula Stuart Mason
Public Relations Officer, National Maritime Museum

The rating stood nervously in front of the commander at the regular 'requestmen and defaulters' in one of our wartime shore establishments.

'Request,' said the petty officer importantly, 'for leave to be present when his wife gives birth to a baby.'

The commander eyed the rating and pondered briefly.

'Request refused,' he said. And to the requestman: 'Jones, I am sorry, but although you may well be very necessary at the laying of the keel, I consider you quite superfluous at the launching.'

Rear Admiral A.J. Whetstone
Assistant Chief of Naval Staff (Operations)

While flag officer sea training at Portland, I spent several hours each day visiting ships at sea to observe the progress of their training. To save time, transfers between ships were generally carried out by helicopters from the Portland Air Station, *HMS Osprey*.

One day, having been winched up without incident from a survey vessel for transfer to another, I was invited to jump out of the helicopter, as the pilot, aware of possible engine failure, had decided to ditch. My initial reaction was that this was Commander Air's revenge for my failure to complete a routine ditching drill the previous week, but with forceful encouragement from the aircrewmen, I took the plunge, followed by my flag lieutenant and the helicopter crew and the aircraft itself. Having inflated my 'mae west' I swam to the rescue dinghy to join the other survivors – nobody had been hurt in the ditching. Once safely aboard I turned to the aircrewman beside me in the dinghy and asked how long it would be before the search and rescue helicopter arrived. 'We were the search and rescue helicopter,' he replied with a wry smile.

The Right Honourable
William F. Deedes
Editor, *Daily Telegraph*

We had hoped to go on D-Day, as the motor battalion supporting 8th Armoured Brigade which was among those assaulting the coast of Normandy. We were crowded out, and had to settle for the West Ham docks on 10 June 1944, where our singular vehicles, American half-track White scout cars were to be loaded in two ships, *S54* and *T37*. Major F.J.R. (Fred) Coleridge, our second in command, later a pillar of Eton, called me urgently. The dockers due to load our cars had a problem. No loading rates had been prescribed for our half-tracks. Without knowing the rate, they said sadly, they couldn't load. We bargained incredulously but amicably. Of no avail. I adopted the tone of Shakespeare's *King Henry IV, Part II*. Some, surely might have their own kin battling to secure the bridgehead. Would they not waive the rate, and speed us forward? The dockers responded enthusiastically. They were absolutely on our side. They wished us all the very best – but, no rate, you see. Impossible!

As a tremendous concession, however, eager to speed the downfall of Hitler, they eventually agreed that our riflemen be allowed to load the cars, 'advised' by a senior docker. It seemed a winning card, until one observed that riflemen with cranes were less reliable than dockers with rifles. The cars went in like spillikins. They had been tenderly waterproofed so that they could run through some depth of water off the landing craft. We crossed our fingers. We sailed (on 13 June). We joined the great armada on 15 June. We were launched with great skill by the Royal Navy. Five of my company's cars, their waterproofing fatally battered on loading, 'drowned' in about three feet of water. It was humiliating, but not the ultimate humiliation. On the beach in front of us, by

106

sad coincidence, were assembled General Montgomery and his staff taking stock of the build-up. It did not seem to me a propitious moment to seek audience and explain that the dockers at West Ham had had a problem with our rates.

Arthur N. Christmas
Former Chief Scientific Officer and Director of Materials Quality Assurance, Ministry of Defence

In the mid-1950s I was attached to the British Defence Staff in Washington DC, USA, and one of my colleagues was a brigadier whom I shall hereafter refer to as Johnnie.

Now Johnnie was not only a loved and respected extrovert but an able and experienced sailor. It was not surprising, therefore, that he was invited by the cadets of the US naval establishment at Annapolis to become a member of their crew in the annual yacht race to Bermuda in the rôle of cook.

Johnnie accepted this invitation on the condition that the 'dry' traditions of the US Navy should not apply to him and that he could arrange his personal stores accordingly.

On the first night out, Johnnie started the meal with a soup, which was much appreciated by the crew.

'What is this delicious soup?' enquired one member.

'Oh,' replied Johnnie, 'it's Scotch Broth.'

And it was!

The Right Reverend J.D. Wakeling
Bishop of Southwell

It may seem odd for a bishop to admit to a criminal offence even if it was committed over forty years ago, but that is, I suppose, what in fact I am doing.

At the time I was a very junior officer serving in a Royal Marine battalion. We were languishing in Freetown, Sierra Leone, where we had been sent as part of an expeditionary force which, with the help of Free French forces, aimed at capturing Dakar. The expedition was a disaster. We never landed at Dakar and serious damage was done to naval units supporting our assault so that the attack was called off. Thereafter we spent nearly six months in Freetown, partly in our floating hotel of a troopship and partly under canvas on shore in malarious circumstances.

Malaria so decimated our battalion that we became unoperational and so it was decided to send us back to England to train for and undertake other seaborne operations.

We were sick and tired of languishing in Freetown and decided that our departure must be marked by a celebration. At the time, on the shores of Lumley beach where we were encamped was the clubhouse of the Freetown Golf Club. Outside it stood a small cannon donated to the club, with a brass plate recording the gift. We decided to take this cannon with us on board our troopship in order to fire a farewell salute as we sailed out of Freetown harbour.

Six of us therefore one night 'fetched' the cannon in a jeep, bringing it to our sick bay in camp where the medical officer, leader of the gang, made a crate to hide its progress on board. The crate proved too big to remove from the place in which it had been built, so the cannon was wrapped in a bundle made up of a marquee which, with many others, was being taken on board with us.

All went well and it arrived on board, though disaster nearly ensued when the dockers on the quay were puzzled that one tent should be so heavy, and in pushing it over the quayside into the lighter were horrified to see it nearly sink the lighter. I can't remember how it got on board except that it was embarked as 'medical stores'.

Once on board the acquisition of the cannon became public knowledge all round the ship, though thankfully not to the members of Freetown Golf Club. The cannon was mounted on deck ready to be fired as we 'crossed the bar'. The MO was busy making a round to fire, something in the nature of a blank shell which would make a lot of noise but no more. All he had was medical stores and cartridges from a twelve-bore shotgun.

As our ship weighed anchor and got under way, every man on board was on deck to witness the firing of the farewell salute. The ship's officers were anxious lest the explosion would damage the new degausing equipment just installed as protection against magnetic mines. At the critical moment the MO fired the cannon. Alas, there was no bang, only a pathetic 'fizz' which reduced us all to helpless mirth. Actually it was a very appropriate conclusion. Like the whole Dakar expedition it went off not with a bang but a whimper.

We decided to give the cannon to the golf club at St Andrews as a present from the Freetown Golf Club, but such were 'the exigencies of the Service' in wartime, it never got there; indeed we never got the cannon ashore. I wish I knew what happened to it.

Dr Magnus Pyke
Scientist, author and broadcaster

My brother-in-law, not by nature a pugnacious man, spent the Second World War in the Royal Navy, where he rose to the rank of lieutenant. Most of his fighting was done in a minesweeper off Iceland. The Germans were interested in my brother-in-law's doings and sent a great big Dornier aeroplane to watch him. They did not try to harm him but flew round and round as he swept.

There was a Bofors gun on the minesweeper and, while the Dornier circled too far off to be hit, the men on the gun followed it round and round to be ready to shoot – just in case.

'This is tedious, sir,' the gunners said to my brother-in-law. 'Can't you do something?'

Always mindful of his men, my brother-in-law instructed his signaller to send a message with his lamp pointed towards the circling enemy.

'CAN YOU SPEAK ENGLISH?'

'YA,' came the answer, flashing back.

'PLEASE FLY ROUND THE OTHER WAY.'

Immediately, the German plane, followed by the British gunners, the signaller and my brother-in-law, began to revolve in the opposite direction.

It may not have been magnificent, but it was war, even if war humanized by the residual civilian remaining under my brother-in-law's naval uniform.

Sir John Moore
Second Crown Estate Commissioner

We had had a busy night chasing E-boats to and fro across a calm and moonlit North Sea. An hour before dawn all went quiet, and I stopped my motor torpedo boat to listen, with the engines cut. After a few minutes, we heard a faint low drone – but clearly not from far away. We had not come across anything like it before. Suddenly, only feet away and coming towards us was the tiny conning tower of a midget submarine (of which craft we had heard intelligence reports only). We crash-started our three huge engines, loosed off a ferocious hail from the only twin machine gun we could bring to bear and skidded into the fastest and smallest circle we could make. The submarine just collided with our stern as we hurled ourselves clear, but we circled tightly and were back only seconds later. The submarine had already sunk. Its two-man crew were splashing in the water. We picked them up. They were young, frightened, cold, wet and desperately tired. But they were the enemy – the first we had seen face to face in five years of war at sea – and had to be reckoned dangerous. They had already done us some mischief in the collision – as yet we knew not what. A motor torpedo boat is small and vulnerable. In some desperation, I ordered that the prisoners be put in the fore-peak – a tiny triangular compartment right up in the bows, with no portholes and only a little circular hatch with a steel cover. It was where we usually kept the buckets and scrubbers and mooring lines. Prisoners could do no harm. I posted a large sentry over the closed hatch, armed him with a tommy gun and a powerful torch and made sure the prisoners saw he was there. We set about the collision damage.

Half an hour later we had all under control and could think of returning to base. Everything went still, while my navigator assessed our position and planned our course. Suddenly I heard a rapid tapping noise from the forepeak. Alarmed and enraged, I concluded that even now my prisoners, desperate to the last, were seeking to cut or chisel their way out. I armed myself with an Aldis lamp and a revolver, and rushed forward, ordering the sentry to fling open the hatch of our forepeak cell and to keep his tommy gun well-trained when I gave the word. The tapping went on. 'Now!' I shouted. We flung back the hatch and shone several thousand candlepower on our prisoners. Their tapping mischief became immediately clear. Their teeth were chattering, hard. . . .

Admiral Sir William Pillar
Commandant, Royal College of Defence Studies

From time to time there break out arguments about how best to mix a dry martini, and sometimes these become widespread. Such an argument was going on at the same time as a committee was making recommendations on how to improve survival kits for use after shipwreck.

One member of the committee suggested that miniature bottles of gin and martini should be included in the kits on the supposition that as soon as the survivor began to mix himself a martini, someone would appear from somewhere to tell him how to do it.

Dr Neil Cossons
Director, National Maritime Museum

Admiral Sir Howard William Kelly was one of the great characters of the navy between the wars. He was known for his strong likes and dislikes and for his quick and sardonic wit, and there was constant speculation in the navy about his prickly relationship with his brother, Admiral Sir John (Joe) Kelly. In one particularly bad patch, the story went that they bumped into each other in Bond Street.

Joe would have walked on, but Howard touched his arm and said, 'Haven't we met somewhere?'

'Have we?', said Joe coldly.

'Well,' said Howard, 'I think your mother knew my father.'

However, in the 1930s Howard Kelly was commander-in-chief on the China station and he was shipwrecked in the Admiralty yacht *Petersfield*. He and his wife and all the crew escaped safely but the yacht was a total loss, for which Kelly was held by some to be responsible.

Joe Kelly cabled his brother: 'Glad you're safe.'

The exasperated Howard cabled back: 'Glad you're glad.'

*   *   *

One of the most amusing of naval autobiographies is Admiral H.H. Smith's *A Yellow Admiral Remembers* in which he tells this tale of seamanship and common sense from his time on the Mediterranean station in the early 1900s:

'Just before Christmas, while the *Pyramus* was lying in Dockyard Creek at Malta, we had a very heavy "Gregale" gale, which lasted for some two or three days, and stopped all

113

communication between the ships and the shore. Our senior engineer happened to be on shore when the "Gregale" started and he had great difficulty in finding a dghaiso man to put him on board the *Pyramus*. At last he persuaded one to have a try, and they shoved off from the Custom House and managed to get across the harbour. When, however, they arrived abreast the *Pyramus*, a tremendous heavy sea was running and just as the dghaiso reached our accommodation ladder she was caught by a huge comber and whirled away towards the Marina. The senior engineer leaped for dear life and landed on the accommodation ladder, and to his surprise he found the dghaiso man was also on the ladder beside him, while the dghaiso was washed up on to the Marina and smashed to pieces.

' "You have lost your dghaiso, José." remarked the senior engineer.

'The dghaiso man spread out his hands and remarked philosophically, "Signor, plenty more dghaisos – no more José." '

The Right Honourable James Callaghan
Member of Parliament

This story was told me when I was serving with the East Indies Fleet in Trincomalee during the Second World War.

Two nineteen-year-old ratings hired a lightweight motor-cle and set off through the jungle on the road to Colombo. They disturbed a small group of elephants, one of whom pursued them down the road. The young men realized that the elephant was gaining on them, and decided the best thing they

could do was to dismount at the next culvert which ran underneath the road to carry away the storm water, and to crawl into it.

The elephant sniffed suspiciously at the abandoned motorbike and then – unluckily – touched the hot exhaust with the tip of his trunk. He trumpeted in anger, and thrust his trunk as far up the culvert as he could to try to reach the two ratings who were cowering underneath. To his frustration, he could not quite reach them. However, he retreated, gathered piles of dead leaves and dust in his trunk, and proceeded to blow all this up the culvert. He repeated this several times until the young ratings were nearly smothered. They had no idea how to escape, and the elephant showed no signs of going away.

Eventually, the local bus approached and pulled up sharply for the angry elephant was blocking the road. He made as if to charge the bus but the bus driver (who was carrying a shotgun) fired several shots in the air, and the elephant decamped.

Then, to everyone's astonishment, there crawled out from the culvert two frightened and very dishevelled young naval ratings, both caked in dust and sweat, picking twigs and leaves out of their hair.

The story ends that they abandoned the motorbike and completed their journey by bus!

The Right Reverend Henry David Halsey
Bishop of Carlisle

As a young RNVR chaplain after the last war had ended, I served on an aircraft carrier. We were not carrying aircraft but were operating as a kind of a troopship repatriating prisoners of war, carrying Australian wives of British servicemen, etc. The most convenient place for Sunday morning service was in the lift well of the hangar, enclosed, as it was, on three sides, with the congregation seated in the hangar itself. I shall never know whether it was by design or accident that one Sunday morning, just as we were about to sing the first hymn, somebody pressed the lift button. So we began rather earlier than any of us had expected to make the steep ascent to heaven. Fortunately the congregation in the hangar were vouchsafed the view of the new Jerusalem coming down out of the heaven when the other button was pressed.

Captain T.A.C. Keay
RNLI Committee of Management

Late in 1941 during the Second World War the two fleet aircraft carriers *HMS Formidable* and *HMS Illustrious* were crossing the Atlantic in company from west to east, following refits in Norfolk, Virginia. They were unaccompanied and travelling fast and zig-zagging.

One night on the bridge at the turnover of the middle to the morning watch aboard *Formidable*, which was the ship astern, the officer of the watch being relieved turned over wrong information as to the revolutions rung on for the main three engines. He passed on revs well below those in use at the time. Shortly after taking over, the officer of the watch of the morning, seeing that *Formidable* was dropping slightly astern of station, ordered what he thought was a small increase in revs. It was in fact a substantial one in view of the false information he had received, and as a consequence the ship surged forward. Before realizing what was happening and being able to take proper avoiding action, *Formidable* dealt *Illustrious* a glancing blow on her stern. Fortunately damage to both ships was slight and there were no casualties.

Following the incident *Illustrious* signalled to *Formidable*, 'If you touch me there again I'll scream!'

Commandant Vonla McBride
Former Director of WRNS

During the war the gates of Kissy Barracks, Sierra Leone, were manned for some months by a young, keen lieutenant, temporarily unfit for sea service. He found the job so devastatingly boring that he amused himself by writing up the day's log as if the barracks were a ship at sea. He engaged hordes of enemy submarines, weathered impossible storms and sighted incredible sea creatures. Perhaps his most fanciful entry in the log was:

0930 – stopped ship
0935 – all padres over the side, the exercise: walking on water
0936 – away sea boat's crew [or, in civilian parlance – launch the lifeboat!]

Vice Admiral Sir Patrick Bayly
Director, Maritime Trust

Many years ago a young officer was appointed sub-lieutenant in a new cruiser which was to be the flagship of the commander-in-chief of the South Africa station. For a hopeful lad this provided an excellent chance of approval and recognition by a very senior officer and who knows what advantage might accrue?

All went well, although it is true that the admiral, a rather

severe and reserved man, never actually indicated any appro-
bation. However praise is not lightly given in the Royal Navy
and 'up to standard' was the best anyone could expect.

One sultry night in the Bight of Benin the sub took over the
middle watch. The ship was steaming at twenty-five knots and
the resultant breeze made the open bridge bearable, but
elsewhere in the ship officers and crew sweltered with ports
and hatches open to catch a passing air. Tropical lightning
played around the horizon but all was peaceful and pitch dark.
Down aft the C-in-C slept in his cabin under an open skylight.
A sentry patrolled the deck above to keep people at a respect-
ful distance and to tend the skylight.

Suddenly the night was split by a blinding flash. In its glare
the officer of the watch saw what looked like Niagara Falls
close off the starboard bow. He instantly called the watch on
deck and the captain and navigating officer to the bridge, but
in a few moments the ship plunged into a deluge of torrential
rain which, fortified by the ship's speed, made it akin to being
sprayed by a fire hose. However the captain's comprehensive
cursing of the sub topped everything.

A telephone rang and the sub groped for it, thankful for a
diversion.

'Officer of the watch speaking.'

'My cabin is flooded. What are you going to do about it?'

'The watch is very busy, sir, but I'll send them as soon as I
can, sir. Who is speaking please?'

'The commander-in-chief. Who is the officer of the watch?'

'Sub-lieutenant Bayly, sir.'

'I thought so.'

An early appointment to the most junior ship on the station
was not unexpected, but the instant horrific mental image of
the commander-in-chief, Vice Admiral Sir Francis Loftus
Tottenham KCB CBE, awash in his bunk is an enduring
memory.

Richard Baker
Broadcaster

Nowadays metal lapel badges with pertinent messages printed on them are commonplace, not least in the Services, where they are often given away as souvenirs. Sometimes, indeed, one comes across the most unlikely recipients of such objects.

In the mid-1970s, as an RNR officer, I was involved in a naval exercise in the Indian Ocean after which our flotilla paid a visit to the island of Mauritius. On the evening of our arrival, a large reception was given on board the flagship, *HMS Tiger*, to which many members of the diplomatic corps in Mauritius were invited, among them the Russian ambassador. In the course of a convivial evening, he naturally met a number of submariners from the nuclear submarine *HMS Dreadnought* which was in company with us.

The following night a party of officers from *Tiger*, including me, were invited to a party at the Soviet Embassy. Under strict orders from our admiral to arrive and leave together, and in no way to act more cordially than correctness demanded, we were all naturally on our best behaviour.

When I was presented to the ambassador, a large, apparently amiable man in a white uniform liberally covered in medals, he asked if I had been to Russia.

'Yes, sir,' I replied, 'I went on a wartime convoy to Murmansk.'

'Ah,' he said. 'Then you must be a friend of Russia!'

'I hope I am, sir,' I said guardedly.

'I will give you a Russian medal,' he announced, apparently satisfied with my answer. Whereupon he plunged his hand into his pocket, pulled out a pile of small medals and pinned one on my uniform.

'Now,' he said, 'I will show you the English medal presented to me yesterday evening.' And turning back the lapel of his uniform, he pointed to the metal disc displayed there. It read: 'SUBMEN ARE SUPER.'

Full marks to *Dreadnought*'s submariners, I thought. But I've never been really sure who won that small exchange in the maritime cold war.

Richard F. Barclay
RNLI Committee of Management

I begged passage with the no. 1 Cromer boat in August or September 1940, when it was being taken from Cromer to Row Hedge for repair. As we passed Yarmouth, we saw an Italian steamer on fire, having been mined, and were then met by a naval trawler who instructed us not to use the inner passage, presumably because of the mining. Instead of going a considerable way round the sands, the coxswain took us straight over. Although we bottomed once or twice in the trough of the waves, we made an uneventful trip, except that we could see tremendous efforts being made to prepare the beach defences against invasion and could hear heavy guns practising.

When we got into Row Hedge a telegram was waiting for the coxswain from a colonel in the Royal Artillery, apologizing for having shelled us with his six-inch guns under the impression that we were a target. Fortunately their accuracy was such that we were quite unaware that they were shooting at us.

121

Admiral Sir William Pillar
Commandant, Royal College of Defence Studies

During a visit to a naval training ship I came across an office door which had on it: 'Engineering Information and Educational Instructor Office'.

I remarked that such a title seemed a bit of a mouthful and was told that the officer concerned had described his job in that way because he had long harboured the ambition, in this age of initials, to pick up his telephone and say, 'EIEIO.'

Maurice Buckmaster
Head of French Section, Special Operations Executive, Second World War

My only 'maritime' experience was on board *HMS Barham* in Dakar harbour in 1940, when *HMS Resolution* was torpedoed and *Barham* took her in tow. All the while the band of the Royal Marines played stirring tunes as the bombs rained down.

Editor's footnote: There is now a lifeboat named *Barham* stationed at Great Yarmouth, Norfolk. She was named by her donor whose brother was one of the 859 who died when *HMS Barham* herself was torpedoed in 1941.

David Aubrey
Honorary Secretary, Port Talbot Lifeboat Station

Some ships' companies on a courtesy visit to Port Talbot were the guests of the local Royal Naval Association Club. There had been a swinging evening and the beer was going down as if there was no tomorrow.

Some of the ship's officers found their way to the bar, the habitat of some very old salts, and the topic of conversation turned to long service and World War Two. 'Who had seen the most action?' they asked. Everyone pointed to Harry, in his usual place by the bar. 'Who had the longest service?' Again all fingers pointed to Harry. 'How long did he serve?' One wag suggested to a very junior officer he might like to ask Harry himself. The officer enquired of the barmaid what Harry drank and made his approach. Harry accepted the drink; after all, this well-educated lad was a guest of the club. Harry answered most of the questions, much to our amazement, but we noticed his patience was wearing a little thin. Then came the sixty-four-thousand-dollar question; 'When did you join, Harry?' We all wanted an answer to this one.

'Well, lad,' he said, looking the officer right in the eyes and without a smile on his face, 'I can't rightly recall, but I will tell you one thing, Nelson was a bastard for leave!'

Harry Barrett
Managing Director, *Fishing News*

Being a policeman of the seas can be an unenviable rôle, but it does have its lighter moments. This is the lot of the Royal Navy Fisheries Protection Squadron, which patrols the waters around our coast on the lookout for poachers.

High on the poaching list is the much-sought-after salmon, and the navy spends a lot of its time seeing that this fish does not get into the wrong hands.

One skipper apprehended by the navy for illegal salmon fishing had his salmon taken aboard a navy ship. An open-and-shut case, one would think!

At the court hearing, the magistrate requested the navy to produce the evidence. A rather embarrassed navy officer shuffled forward to tell the court that his crew had eaten it.

Gamekeeper turned poacher!

Case dismissed!

Admiral Sir William Pillar
Commandant, Royal College of Defence Studies

Our captain was a distinguished, highly decorated submariner but he had never served in a destroyer before. As was the custom in those days, very shortly after sailing from our home ports for the first time, the whole squadron was engaged in high-speed manoeuvres.

Going on to the compass platform, I saw the captain standing fairly well back while the sub-lieutenant conned the ship.

I said, 'Good morning, sir. How's it going?'

He replied, 'I've no idea! It strikes me you just have to grit your teeth and hang on.' Then, looking forward and seeing another ship crossing our bows at thirty knots only a short distance ahead, he said, 'Mind you, I do sometimes feel like turning round and saying "Flood Q [a submarine's main ballast tank]. Take her down!"'

John Corin
Penlee and Penzance Branch, RNLI

The admiral was extraordinarily keen on his laundry and had special arrangements in Valletta. On entering harbour, after a long spell at sea, the flagship signalled, 'Please send admiral's woman.' There was a certain amount of alarm and consternation ashore and the hope that the admiral's wife could not read signals. However a correction came very quickly from the flag bridge: 'To my last signal – insert "washer" between Admiral and woman.'

Rear Admiral D.W. Haslam
Hydrographer of the Navy

Being driven in my ship's Land Rover across London, our engine stalled right in the centre of Oxford Circus. My uniformed leading seaman driver jumped out and was cranking the starting handle round and round without any success (it was an old car and long ago) when a bus driver – blocked by our vehicle – leaned out of his cab and called out, 'What's the matter, Jack, can't you get the anchor up?'

Admiral Sir John Fieldhouse
First Sea Lord

A true story. The commander at his defaulters' table asked a rating who was charged with being 'absent over leave' why he was late returning to the ship.

The man replied, 'Well, sir, I was with this young lady and when I woke up and looked out of the window at the clock it was only 5.15. So I went back to sleep. When I woke up again it was still showing 5.15 so I jumped up but still got back too late.'

'Had the clock stopped?' asked the commander.

'To be honest, sir,' replied the sailor, 'it was a petrol pump.'

Sir John Moore
Second Crown Estate Commissioner

The sun was over the yardarm in the dock which was the home
of my MTB flotilla. After a night at sea and a morning spent
getting ready for the next night, my crew were following the
long-established tradition of 'having their tot' of rum. The
rules ought to have ensured that one tot per day was all that
anyone got. The unsteady merriment of the sailors on the
upper deck suggested all too clearly that King's Rule and
Admiralty Instructions, not to mention Admiralty Fleet
Orders, had been ignored.

'Coxswain,' I thundered, 'what is all this?'

'Sir . . .' he said, drawing himself to that over-rigid attempt
at the position of attention enforced by drink, 'Sir . . .' and he
saluted with excessive decorum, 'Sir . . .' (and this in a tone of
voice which indicated that he was about to declare a resound-
ing and eternal truth, of total conviction and to which there
could be no answer) '. . . we are celebrating . . . the anniversary . . . of the ship's gramophone.'

Admiral Sir William Pillar
Commandant, Royal College of Defence Studies

A young naval officer – a keen team man – had just taken command of his first ship, and to expound his philosophy he cleared lower deck and addressed the ship's company.

He said, 'This is not my ship. She is not your ship. She is OUR ship.'

And from well forward a voice was heard to say, 'Good! Let's sell her!'

Many Cargoes

Tankers, tradesmen and tramps

Dr Ronald Hope
Director, Marine Society

The marine superintendent was bawling out the deck cadet for lack of diligence in his studies.

'I suppose it's the old story, Jones,' he opined. 'The fool of the family sent to sea!'

'Oh, no, sir,' replied the cadet. 'I don't think so, sir! Things have changed since your day, sir.'

Commander R. D. Wall
Former Deputy Director, Maritime Trust

The young third mate of a small freighter bound out of the English Channel 'forgot' to alter course after bringing Wolf Rock abeam and found himself among some distinctly rocky islets. He put out a panic call for the master who, while in the midst of sorting things out on the bridge, heard stentorian hailing from the direction of the port waterline. Peering down through the dawn mist from the wing of the bridge, he discerned a fishing boat with a piratical-looking crew of two.

'What's that?' he yelled.

'I said, "D'you need a Scilly pilot?"' came the answer.

'No, I b— well don't,' roared the exasperated master, 'I've got enough silly b—s in this vessel already.'

Dr Denis Rebbeck
Former Chairman, Harland and Wolff, Shipbuilders

A few years ago when we were out with the Sunnyland Beagles in County Down, we finished up near the village of Comber and it was suggested we visit the local pub named the 'First and Last'.

As we stood at the bar, all covered in mud and dirt, a man approached me (he had obviously spent all day in the pub and was rather the worse for drink). The following conversation then took place:

'I know you,' he said.

'Yes, we may well have met before!'

'Ah, but sir, we did, you know.'

'Where and when?'

'On the Victoria Wharf in the Belfast Shipyard in 1948.'

'Good gracious, how on earth can you remember that?'

'Ah, but I can,' he said. 'I can very easily for as we stood talking all those years ago a big seagull came along and shat on your bowler hat!'

* * *

At the launch of the lightship tender *Grannaile* for the commissioners of Irish lights at the A. & J. Inglis Shipyard in Glasgow in 1948, the sponsor was a veritable amazon of a woman (appropriately named Miss Guinness!) who literally hurled the bottle of champagne from the stand at the poor unsuspecting little ship, whereupon Sir John Craig, then chairman of Colvilles, the Scottish steelmakers, leaned over to me and said, 'Dr Rebbeck, someone should have warned your lassie that the hull plating is only mild steel.'

Two Belfast Shipyard workers, fishing off Bangor in County Down, were hauling the fish in fast and one said, 'I wish we could find this spot again.' That was agreed upon but the question was how to do it.

One man said, 'We could put an X on the boat in white paint.'

'No,' the other said, 'that would never do.'

'Why not?' the first man enquired.

'Well, you see,' retorted his companion, 'next time we might not get the same boat!'

* * *

A small Clyde coaster was steaming up the Clyde, flat out, at about seven knots in a pea-soup fog. The captain was anxious to reach Greenock before the pubs shut but, knowing he was in the wrong, steaming so fast in such a thick fog, he posted the mate up in the fo'castle and told him to look ahead and report anything he might see.

Every now and then the captain would shout from the bridge, 'Mr McGregor, can you see anything?'

'No, captain, nothing,' was the sullen answer.

This went on for about an hour. The mate, cold and bitter, was becoming very fed up, so when the captain again enquired, 'Mr McGregor, can you see anything?' he answered, 'Yes, captain, I can see a seagull.'

The captain, however, not easily pushed aside, shouted, 'Tell me, Mr McGregor, is it swimming or walking, because if it's walking I'll ease her back a wee bit.'

Sir Ralph Richardson
Actor

'I am not well, unable to be on bridge,' said the captain of the splendid ship. 'I must leave everything to you.' The noble captain sank back on his pillow and seemed to pass off to sleep.

For many months the commander had entered the cabin at this time of the morning. He had always seen the captain brisk and cheerful, finishing his dressing; though every morning he had seen him do one strange thing – he would stop suddenly, take from his neck a slender silver chain on which there was a key, go over to his desk, unlock a drawer, draw out a single paper which he would study for a second, then relock the drawer.

This had always puzzled the commander, and now, as he looked at his captain lying there, he saw the silver chain around his neck. He leant forward and slipped off the chain and, unlocking the drawer, drew out the paper. On it was written, 'Port is left, starboard is right.'

John Corin
Penlee and Penzance Branch, RNLI

In 1595 a Spanish raiding party burnt Paul, Penzance and Newlyn, the last being now the location of Penlee lifeboat station. The raid had the effect of delaying the start of Drake's last expedition and causing it to go off at half-cock.

In due course the burnt-out church of St Pol de Leon at Paul was rebuilt, but fire marks can still be seen. A few years ago funds were needed for repairs, and the Parochial Church Council had the nerve to write to the Spanish ambassador asking for a contribution, as some compensation for the damage way back. The letter was most diplomatically composed. The ambassador's reply was full of courtly grace. A contribution of £50 was included with a gentle reminder that Drake and his lads had a habit of burning and pillaging Spanish churches and any reciprocal gestures would be appreciated!

Sir Terence Beckett
Director-General, CBI

On the bridge of the small mail-steamer from Glasgow, en route to the west coast, stood the captain and a couple of lady schoolteachers whom he had invited up there. Noticing the approach of a heavy shower of rain, the captain shouted down the 'voice pipe' to the crew member in charge of the saloon bar below: 'Is there a big mackintosh down there that would cover two ladies?'

The answer came back: 'No, but there's a wee MacGregor here that's prepared to try.'

* * *

Two retired sea-captains were sitting in deck-chairs overlooking the topless bathers on Brighton beach, recalling their experiences aboard ship during the First World War.

The first one said, 'George, you know those pills they gave us just before we put out to sea; you know, the ones they told us would help keep our minds off the girls?'

'Now you mention it, I think I do remember those pills. Why do you ask?'

'Well,' said the first retired captain, 'I think they're beginning to work.'

Austin Mitchell
Member of Parliament

The Humber Bridge has made going to foreign parts like Hull a lot easier and quicker but it's killed a lot of local humour, fun and fury, and particularly the following joke which is known as Grimsby No. 1 Joke, taken from the Grimsby Bumper Fun Book, 1908.

A young Lincolnshire lass, pining away in her village, was filled with a romantic desire to escape to Australia. But how to do it from Lincolnshire? Buoyed with hope, she set out to the Gateway to the World and there in Grimsby met a sailor, plied him with drink and got him to promise to take her to Australia by hiding her away in his cabin. But there was a snag. She had to share his bunk. Reluctantly she agreed. That night she was smuggled on to the ship.

Next day the voyage began and with it the unremitting sexual attentions of the voracious sailor. Day and night, night and day. Until she could stand no more. There was no turning back. She would face discovery. It couldn't be as bad as what she was having to face already. Distraught, exhausted, dishevelled, she staggered up to the deck to bump straight into the captain.

'Forgive me. I'm a stowaway. How far from Australia are we now?' she sobbed.

'Australia?' said the captain. 'Why, lass, this is the Grimsby-to-Hull ferry.'

John Archer

Managing Director, International Tanker Owners'
Pollution Federation, formerly Marine Division,
Department of Trade

Two old mariners were standing on Westminster Bridge looking at debris floating in the river.

'See that piece of wood there, that big one? I reckon that must be the Board of Trade,' said one.

After a pause, 'No, I don't reckon so,' said the other. 'It's big enough, but it's moving downstream too fast.'

Captain George King

Chairman, Marine Society

The captain was short, square, formidable and given to outbursts of navigation. One evening he, the chief officer and fourth officer took evening stars. As the cadet on watch, I recorded the chronometer times for them. Fifteen minutes later the chief officer had completed his calculations, plotted his intercepts on the Sumner chart and retired discreetly to the front of the bridge. In the chartroom the captain toiled on. In a further fifteen minutes the fourth officer had worked out his sights and awaited the call to plot them. The captain continued to toil on. Fifty minutes from sight time, as I returned to the chartroom sent on some errand, he flung his pencil violently on the table, slammed his sight book shut and stumped off the bridge, snarling as he went, 'Navigation is *not* an exact science, boy.'

James Herriot
Author

As a country vet, my maritime experiences are limited, but I do remember one occasion vividly. It was in the autumn of 1961 and I was asked to accompany a cargo of valuable pedigree sheep to Russia. I was to be their veterinary attendant and ensure that they arrived at their destination in good condition, and since their value in modern terms must have been around £150,000 it was a very real responsibility. But the whole venture was attractive as a change from my normal life in practice in the Yorkshire Dales and I accepted eagerly.

I was surprised to find that the cattle ship was quite tiny – about 300 tons – and when we ran into force nine gales in the Baltic the little vessel was thrown around like a cork. I will never forget that night. I lay sleepless, jamming my arms and legs against the sides of the bunk as my suitcase, money, books, pipe and tobacco flew about the cabin and a deafening banging and clattering rose from all over the ship.

At dawn I looked out on a tossing grey waste of water, the wind howled and rain dashed against the cabin window. This was depressing but the effect on my precious sheep was much worse. Nearly all the big Romney Marsh rams were in a desperate plight, many prostrate, others staggering about, fighting desperately for breath, their mouths gaping and frothing. They all looked as if they were certainly going to die, and I suppressed a rising panic at the thought that my entire assignment was doomed. What were the Russians going to think when I presented them with a heap of carcases?

I had a very limited supply of medicines with me but among them was the wonder drug – new in those days – called cortisone. The brand name was Predsolan and it was one of the first of the steroid products. I had never used it for anything like this acute, storm-induced stress, but I had nothing else. I gave all the affected sheep an injection.

The result was magical. Within two hours the animals were normal. I had never seen such a spectacular recovery. A tragedy had been averted.

I have been privileged to be one of the generation of veterinary surgeons who lived through the period in practice when the antibiotics, steroids and other new drugs brought about a revolution in our methods of treating animal diseases.

During those years I learned many lessons, but the one which sticks in my mind is the one I learned at sea.

Dr Ronald Hope
Director, Marine Society

Winston Churchill was an Elder Brother of Trinity House. Shortly after the First World War he appeared at Versailles wearing the cap and jacket which are peculiar to the Elder Brethren when dressed for official occasions. Clemenceau asked what uniform he was wearing and Churchill is said to have replied, in somewhat inadequate French, 'Je suis un frère ainé de la Trinité.'

'Mon Dieu!' exclaimed Clemenceau. 'Quelle influence!'

Sir Robert Mark
Former Commissioner, Metropolitan Police

When I was at Sandhurst we spent seven weeks on general infantry training before moving on to the more sophisticated instruction necessary to command three tanks. The troop in its last week always did a combined exercise with the infantry on Thursley Common. All this was interspersed by ruthless physical training, one incident of which deserves recounting. We had done a three or four miles' run and walk, involving a little way crawling underground and some swarming across ropes between trees. The final stage was to swim the 'back' lake. This was not the ornamental lake in front of the college but an evil-looking narrow stretch of dirty and deep water behind the college. We were wearing steel helmets, boots, denims but were not carrying rifles. We did this in tank crews of five and as the old man of my crew I brought up the rear. To my horror, on leaving the raft in the middle of this horrible pool I got acute cramp in both hands for the first time in my life. I daren't cry out, because lack of moral fibre was the shortest route to RTU (returned to unit). I decided to complete the swim by backstroke but as soon as I turned over my helmet filled with water and began to pull my head back. I bobbed up and down for a moment or two until I realized that I really was in trouble. At that point I lost my moral fibre but I was twelve inches under water and it therefore did me neither good nor harm. I remember at the end feeling a moment or two of intense fear, pushing my helmet forward over my head and seeing it swirl away into a murky cloud, and suddenly all fear left me. I can only remember thinking ' . . . it!' and then passing out. As luck would have it, a member of my troop who was off duty happened to be sunbathing at the side of the lake. His name was Stanley Dwyer, and he was a fellow Mancunian employed by Thomas Hedley, the Trafford Park soap people. He also happened to be a superb and powerful swimmer. Sensing something wrong, he did a long underwater dive, seized me by the cross-straps of my equipment and hoisted me to the surface, where he held on to the raft until help came. When I woke up I was being pumped clean of the filth and slime I had swallowed. As soon as I looked alive I was told to 'get fell in'. The following morning the squadron sergeant major addressed me in no uncertain manner. 'Squadron leader's orders 0900 hours. The charge, by neglect, carelessly losing a steel helmet, the property of His Majesty, whilst on active service.' I just replied, 'Sir.' I was learning. The squadron leader was an elegant Grenadier major called Gregory Hood, who had won an MC in Norway. As we stood in front of him the sergeant major said, 'Sir! The officer cadet pleads "Not Guilty". 'E produces this eight-figure map reference. It denotes precisely where the steel 'elmet is. It is beyond 'is physical means to recover it.' Whereupon Gregory Hood, without lifting his head from the papers he was reading, said,

'Not guilty. Ordered to pay nine shillings and sixpence, the cost of one steel helmet.' Thus was military protocol satisfied and the books balanced. In fact I never got a replacement until I was commissioned and bought one from the regimental quartermaster. I only tell this story because it has a postscript. In 1976 I was lecturing at the Staff College as Commissioner of Police of the Metropolis. At the end of the session the curtains behind me suddenly drew apart and there stood the commandant, Sir Hugh Beach. He said, 'Commissioner. We have heard of your tribulations and think it is about time that Sandhurst made amends.' He then walked forward bearing a cushion on which rested a steel helmet, which is now one of my treasured possessions, though honesty compels me to confess that it was not the one I lost.

From *In the Office of Constable* (William Collins)

Captain David Sinclair
Honorary Secretary, Thurso Lifeboat Station

During 1948, a tanker trading between the Far East and the Persian Gulf ports was approaching the entrance to the Gulf of Oman. The chief officer was on watch as dawn broke. A first-year apprentice, Robinson, was also on watch, and as the visibility was poor he was keeping a lookout, in addition to the man on the fo'c'sle head.

Suddenly, an ancient dhow loomed out of the misty stillness. There was a loud clump – not much more.

The chief officer shouted to the apprentice, 'Robinson, tell the captain what has happened,' and dashed to the engine-room telegraph.

143

Dutifully, Robinson entered the captain's cabin, rushing through the dayroom and into the sleeping quarters.

'Excuse me, sir, excuse me.'

'Yes, boy. What's the matter?'

'I think we have touched a dhow, sir.'

'Think, boy? Don't you know?'

'Yes, sir, I saw it.'

'Tell me more, Robinson.'

'Well, sir, one half has floated down the starboard side and the other half down the port side!'

Footnote: The survivors were rescued.

Dr Ronald Hope
Director, Marine Society

At one time most ships' engineers were Scots. One chief engineer is said to have greeted a new applicant for a junior post with the words, 'Are ye a mechanic?'

The reply came: 'Naw, I'm a McTavish.'

'A'reet,' was the reply. 'The job's yours.'

* * *

Captain Vine, one-time captain superintendent of the now defunct Prince of Wales Sea Training School in Dover, had been a *Worcester* cadet. He used to relate how on his first morning on board his first ship he gave the captain a smart salute and said, 'Good morning, sir.' The following morning he did the same. The ship had been in fog all night and the captain, of course, had spent the night on the bridge. He replied: 'Good morning, good morning, good morning, Vine. And let that do for the whole bloody voyage.'

In similar circumstances another shipmaster in reply to a cadet's cheery 'Good morning, sir,' is said to have growled, 'When I want a weather report I'll ask for it.'

Sir Robin Gillett
Former Lord Mayor of London;
Elder Brother, Trinity House

Captain Jones was truly, in his own mind and that of his crew, 'master under God'.

One day a burial at sea was necessary, and, due to an unforeseen emergency requiring his presence on the bridge, the captain delegated the mate to commence the proceedings. Situation under control, he arrived on the scene as the mate was pronouncing the words, 'I am the resurrection and the life.'

Snatching the prayer book from his hands, the good captain entoned, 'No, Mister Mate, *I* am the resurrection and the life.'

Max Bygraves
Entertainer

When I was a kid, we had an old cork lifebelt, the type used in those old pre-war movies, the kind that extras sang 'Abide With Me' in, the sort the hero handed to an old lady with a line like "Ere, love, you need it more than me.' This lifebelt had been fished out of the Surrey Commercial Docks in London by my father and hung in the passage of our council flat, which had so much damp he probably figured that one day the family would need it quickly.

My father had been a professional boxer but at thirty he was too old for the fight game and was one of the full-time unemployed, sometimes getting work as a casual docker. If the work wasn't there, he drew dole and spent all his spare time thinking up inventions that would make him, he hoped, if not rich, at least able to get off that degrading dole queue.

At that time, in the early 1930s, one of the greater scientific breakthroughs was an eight-hour battery. This meant that as long as we could raise the cost, which was fourpence, us kids could ride our bicycles into the dark evenings and not be jumped on by Old Bill, who was very fond of doing so and making us fork out a five-shilling fine to Mrs Campion, the magistrate at Tower Bridge police station.

One evening I came home from school and found dad with the lifebelt across his knees and my bicycle lamp mounted on it with sticking plaster. He was most excited. He had hit on the idea of scooping out some of the cork, inserting the lamp with an eight-hour battery, so making it possible for people in the sea at night to be seen from long distances.

A few days later I walked with him to an office in the City where he hoped to show his invention and be rewarded, but a large commissionaire told him he'd have to forward it by post with complete details.

He never got round to posting it off because he was never able to afford the postage, and a long time afterwards he read that a similar idea had been thought up. Till the day he died, he wondered if that commissionaire had 'nicked' his idea.

John Corin
Penlee and Penzance Branch, RNLI

The master of a certain vessel was very proud of his ability to determine his position in thick weather, anywhere around the coast of Britain, from a bottom sample obtained by arming the lead. One day, approaching port in a thick fog, he gave orders for a cost of the lead. The Scottish chief engineer was hanging about the deck, impatient to get into port, and the delay increased that animosity which sometimes existed between Scots engineers and English masters. As the lead, with its sample, was brought past him, he seized it from the sailor and wiped his best shore-going boots very thoroughly on it. After this expression of feeling the indignant rating carried on up to the bridge with the lead.

The master examined the lead, sniffed it and, to the covert amazement of others on the bridge, seemed baffled. Then his face cleared and he pronounced, 'Gentlemen, we are now at the corner of Sauchiehall and Argyll Street.'

Dr Ronald Hope
Director, Marine Society

The Reverend Eric Casson, a much-loved Missions to Seamen padre, was a professional seafarer in the Blue Funnel line before he entered the Church. As a young chief officer he was on watch one evening when the captain came up to the bridge.

The captain said, 'Well, mister,' for such was the customary mode of address in the 1930s, 'when will we raise Ushant?'

The mate replied, 'With God's help, sir, we should see the light in half an hour.'

'Very well,' said the captain, turning to go down to his cabin, 'but if God should let us down, mister, be sure to let me know.'

*　*　*

The young cadet, barely sixteen and small for his age, was admiring himself in his smart new uniform, glancing at his reflection in all the shop windows as he walked along. Near the docks he saw two sailors go into a public house.

'I've never done that,' he thought and, looking sideways again at his reflection, he decided to take the risk.

He asked for half a pint of bitter. The barmaid looked him up and down and said, 'Look, sonny, are you after getting me into trouble?'

The cadet paused for a moment and then replied, 'Well, I'll have the bitter first.'

R. M. Linley-Munro
Chief Officer, *SS Opalia*

It's not as though we ever met. But back in 1976 I established that certain rapport that only seafarers can comprehend.

I was mate on a seventy-thousand-tonne tanker and she was on a forty-foot steel yacht with her husband and young child. Southbound from Liverpool to Libya in heavy weather, we had passed Finisterre before I heard her request for a radio check. It was a lousy evening and I was happy to answer her call, only to find myself engaged for almost four hours with a female possessing obvious seamanlike qualities. They had been bound from Brittany to Madeira when they were struck by lightning and seemingly lost all communications. My response to their general call was the first they had heard for two days while hove to and 'lost'.

My response was obviously reassuring to her and conversation ranged from port facilities on the south coast to favourite recipes. I soon realized that she was reluctant to release this tenuous contact with the outside world. With our radios on low power, communication was still possible and we could give them a circle of position of some twenty miles radius. After some deliberation with the radio officer, our medium-frequency transmission was received by the yacht on a hand-held transistor radio, and the ferrite rod aerial gave a rough bearing of north/south, along with a good soaking for the husband, caught on deck when the yacht shipped a heavy sea.

Half an hour later we detected a small echo on our radar bearing, due south at eight miles range, and altered course to pass close by. With our deck lights on to aid recognition, the husband took another soaking before she reported that we were in sight. The delight in her voice was obvious.

Further positional information was exchanged, though we were unable to meet the husband's request for a case of beer, and with little else left to us but to say goodbye, our last request was for a postcard from Madeira to tell us of their safe arrival. We closed down with a message to Portishead radio and broadcast one ourselves to advise of the yacht's position.

Three months later, we still had no news but dismissed this as being symptomatic of the postal system. However an enquiry at Lloyds revealed that the yacht had foundered just one day after our brief encounter and that husband, wife and child had been rescued by a Spanish fisherman.

I don't even know her name, and I never did get my postcard.

Captain George King
Chairman, Marine Society

Between the wars there was a chandler's ship in Birkenhead, run by a man called Arthur Rusby, where seamen could outfit themselves cheaply before joining an outwardbound ship. An assistant presided at a counter on the ground floor, calling the orders up to the proprietor on the warehouse floor above. The items were then delivered to the counter by a chute. On one occasion the assistant was heard to yell, 'Ten bob's wurt' of fireman's gear, Art'ur – and don't put so many wais'coats in this time!'

Sir Barrie Heath
Former Chairman, GKN Ltd

Noah had just hammered the last nail into the ark when he decided to have a practice to see if he could get all the animals stowed away safely. He sounded his trumpet and got them all up from the surrounding district and told them that he could only take two of each species – a male and a female. After they had sorted themselves out he talked to those lucky animals that were going on the great voyage with him. He said, 'This is going to be a difficult journey and animals must be on their best behaviour. There must be no fighting, no fooling around and certainly no hanky-panky.' He explained that this was a test to see if they could all be fitted in. They followed him in two by two and eventually the doors were closed tight and there was just about enough room for the lot of them. He then told them to go outside as he wanted to talk to them in the open. So they all came out laughing and shouting, and he said, 'So far, so good. But the behaviour was not all that I would have liked. I have observed a number of cases of hanky-panky going on in the hold of the ark, and in order to prevent such an occurrence when the journey starts I will arrange for a cloakroom to be available at the top of the gangplank and every male animal will check in his "courting tackle" and he will get a cloakroom ticket in return.' There was a great moan from all the animals and he told them that if they didn't like it they would have to swim.

Eventually the great day came and at the sound of the trumpet they all arrived at the ark, the rain pouring down upon them. They came up the gangplank and cloakroom tickets were issued as arranged. They had a terrible journey and were tossed around inside the ark, but eventually they grounded and everything went quiet.

Mrs Monkey woke Mr Monkey and told him to climb up the inside of the hull and see what he could see outside through the planks. He came down and said that the sun was just coming out and he could see a beautiful cedar tree appearing through the receding waters, and he said, 'My dear, as soon as Mr Noah opens the doors I am going to take you out and take you up into that cedar tree and make love to you in the most fantastic way.'

Mrs Monkey put her little paws on her hips and said, 'Oh, yes! You were no good before you came on the ark and have done nothing except lie in the bilge being sick all the time and now you tell me this silly story.'

He said, 'My dear. You are wrong, and there is something you don't know, and that is that *I* have got the donkey's cloakroom ticket.'

Leslie Crowther
Actor

A: I went out with a girl last night.

B: You went out with a girl last night?

A: Yes, I went out with a girl last night. She was a model. Do you know what her vital statistics were?

B: No.

A: 38 – 22 – 36.

B: That's nothing.

A: Well it looked all right to me!

B: Never mind that. I went out with a girl last night. She was a mermaid. Do you know what her vital statistics were?

A: No.

B: 38 – 22 – and 4/6 a pound!

Brian Rix
Actor-Manager

My grandfather, Robert Rix, had been a ship's master and became a ship-owner with one very small boat. He had three sons, John Robert, Ernest Bertie and my father, Herbert Dobson (Grandma, having married a Bert, was determined to keep it in the family), and all three went into the business, via the sea. JR became a master, EB an engineer and my father went to Trinity House but because he was the youngest and good at maths he was taken straight into the office in Hull.

My father was also mainly responsible for starting a highly successful company known by the splendid title The Dry-pool Dry Dock & Engineering Company Ltd, now known, typically, as The Dry-pool Group. Most of my family were shareholders and once, when I was a 'success' and my father, as chairman, wished to show me off, I was wheeled along to the AGM. It was a rubber-stamp affair for the old man was supposed to read his report and that was, more or less, it. The meeting was attended by my uncles as directors, and JR was then a huge old Yorkshireman of eighty-seven supported on a tripod. His elder son, Kenneth, was sixty-two and sat beside me in the body of the hall. After my father had read his report he asked if there were any questions.

'Why is the dividend only twelve and a half per cent?' enquired sixty-two-year-old Kenneth.

'You bloody shut up, Ken,' said his eighty-seven-year-old father, and Kenneth hurriedly sat down. That was the end of question time.

From *My Farce from My Elbow* (Martin Secker & Warburg)

Dr Ronald Hope
Director, Marine Society

Three retired captains were having a drink together at the Master Mariners Club and bemoaning the fact that they were growing old.

'I'm going deaf,' said the first. 'I often have to ask my wife to repeat things. It's a dreadful business.'

'Well,' said the second, 'at least you're not so bad as I am. I can't even read the telephone directory without borrowing my wife's glasses. It won't be long before I'm blind.'

'But the worst thing,' said the third, 'the worst thing of all, is losing your memory. Only this morning I turned over to my wife in bed and said, "Honey, let's make love." And she replied, "But George, you've just made love." It's terrible when you can't remember things any more.'

Captain George King
Chairman, Marine Society

The ship with the Greek name from *The Odyssey* had been built to last, in 1911. In 1943 the commodore of a convoy which took three weeks from Liverpool to Freetown flew his flag in her. At the end of the passage, as she led the other ships in line-ahead towards the naval control at the harbour entrance, the captain turned to the commodore on the bridge and said, with modest pride, 'D'you know, commodore, this ship is thirty-two years old.'

In the quiet, assured accents of the Britannia Royal Naval College the commodore replied, 'And she looks every minute of it, sir.'

David Aubrey
Honorary Secretary, Port Talbot Lifeboat Station

Cardiganshire skippers were well known in the days of sail, hard but fair, generally God-fearing, and total abstainers. Some time ago, while doing some research, I came up with this true story.

There was one Cardiganshire skipper who had a regular run for his schooner from Wales to Canada and Newfoundland. He was a hard man, permitting no hard drink or bad language aboard, and every Sunday in port or at sea he read to the crew passages from the Bible.

The skipper had for his first mate one Bute Francis, whose nickname pronounced him a Cardiff man. He had been a master in his own right but had fallen from favour because of his love for strong drink. Sober, the skipper knew Bute was the best in the business, but he despised him for his drinking and for having no love for the good book. The skipper only had to detect the smell of rum when Bute was about and he would log him, telling Bute that it was for the good of his soul to be punished thus.

One day, ashore in Newfoundland, the skipper was taken ill with a fever, and, too weak to stand, he was tied in his bunk. The ship sailed on the morning tide with Bute in command. After clearing harbour he went below to fill in the log. Sitting for a while deep in thought, he then took up the pen and wrote:

'18 May 1868. Today the captain was sober . . .'

Richard F. Barclay
RNLI Committee of Management

As a boy in the early days of the war I had a term off from school as I had been ill, and spent most of it with Coxswain Henry Blogg and the fishing fraternity at Cromer.

My family have always called me by my Christian name, Richard, and never used the nickname Dick, but the fishermen began to call me Dick, which I did not much like. One day when I was with Henry Blogg, I blurted this out and asked whether he could tell the fishermen to call me Richard. He looked at me with amused quizzical eyes and said, 'Okay, Peter,' so I have since put up with any nicknames that have come my way.

*   *   *

The frigate I was in had a refit in Auckland, New Zealand, early in 1946 and our petty officers made friends ashore with a rather fast set of girls who proved very expensive! After the refit, we had a couple of days at sea shaking down into normal routine again. The petty officers were extremely relieved to get away from Auckland, and looked forward to a quiet sporting weekend at the small port of Omaru in the South Island. Approaching the South Island from the east at first light, we saw, at least a hundred miles away, the peaks of the whole length of the Southern Alps projecting pink, high into the sky. It was a brilliant sight which faded as the light grew stronger. We duly docked there early in the morning and, to the POs' horror, they saw awaiting them on the quay all their Auckland girlfriends – they had persuaded a friendly Dakota pilot to carry the lot of them to Omaru for the weekend!

Captain George King
Chairman, Marine Society

For well over a century Indian and Chinese seamen have been enormously important in the ships of many British shipping companies. Those privileged to have sailed with them know they have many endearing peculiarities, not least their idiosyncratic use of language. When very young I was momentarily mystified on the occasion that the Indian lookout telephoned the bridge in great excitement and reported, 'Sahib, steam chicken sahib – port side,' and with that a low-flying Coastal Command Hudson roared over the ship.

* * *

In one ship we had a Chinese carpenter called Ah Tong who looked like a Macao pirate but was the most wonderful craftsman and loyal shipmate. I thought I had mastered his staccato delivery until the day, with the ship in dry-dock in the Tyne, he came up to my cabin in a state of agitation and reported, 'No Sunderland water in the lumber trees, Mr Mate.' It took some time to establish that there was no sanitary water in the lavatories.

And then I had a friend who claimed that the cheerful Shanghai storekeeper in his ship was wont to claim, '*Everything* have got – but monkey eggs *no* have got.'

* * *

...my favourite Chinese story concerned a decent, pleasant and very English third engineer called May – 'Cobbley' May from Tiverton (which has nothing to do with the story). Thinking himself alone in the engineroom one day and protected by the machinery noises with the ship steaming at full speed, he broke wind, privately if not quietly. From nowhere the Chinese no. 1 fireman materialized, remarking in his inscrutable Chinese way, 'Me think your belly plenty happy, Number Three; your backside makee plenty sing-song.'

Captain C. R. Kelso
Chief Marine Superintendent, Cayzer, Irvine Shipping Ltd

Travelling home on leave by train, the chief engineer was intrigued by a tiny metal device in the ear of the man sitting opposite. Noting the chief's interest, the man withdrew the device from his ear and displayed the tiny sphere in the palm of his hand.

'Japanese technology,' he volunteered. 'The smallest hearing aid in the world. Would you believe me if I told you that it contains forty-two diodes, a moving coil microphone and a ferromagnetic diaphragm?' Replacing it in his ear, he awaited the reaction.

'Marvellous!' said the chief. 'Was it expensive?'

'Certainly,' said his travelling companion, glancing at his watch. 'It is precisely twenty past three.'

Sir John Moore
Second Crown Estate Commissioner

In a Fairmile motor launch 112 feet long, my duty was to act as a kind of sheepdog and lifeboat at the rear of an east coast convoy of nearly fifty small ships. Because the channel which was swept clear of the many mines in the North Sea was only one mile wide, the ships had to form two long columns, each of some two dozen ships. That meant that the tail was at least three miles, and sometimes five, behind the leading ships. If each ship simply kept pointed at the one ahead, a cross-tide could take the tail well outside the swept channel. This was something I had constantly to watch.

Shortly after midnight in a cold December, one of the stragglers was well out of position. I slid across and called him on my loudhailer.

'Captain, you are nearly a mile to the east of the swept channel. Please move across.'

He gave two short toots on his whistle in acknowledgment – and promptly blew up on a mine. It took us five hours to pull six heavy and helpless men to safety from the floating and oily debris.

Lord Walston

Former Parliamentary Under-Secretary of State
for the Foreign Office

In the mid-1960s, when I was a minister in the Foreign Office, one of the areas for which I had some responsibility was Vietnam, then increasingly involved in war. On one occasion when I visited the country I was taken to a provincial town close to the front. While there the authorities were very anxious that I should visit an area where certain activities were going on which they wished me to see. Although it was not an island it could only be approached by water so we embarked on a smelly and not particularly seaworthy launch, followed in another similar craft by a bevy of journalists. On arriving at our destination it was found that the launch drew too much water to enable us to disembark dry-footed. However, to enable me to do so, those who had gathered on the shore to welcome us went into the nearby infants' school and brought out all the children's benches which they made into an impromptu jetty. I happen to suffer from a disease of the middle ear, as a result of which I have no balance. I knew that if I attempted to walk on the benches I would inevitably fall into the water. I therefore took off my shoes and socks and rolled up my trousers and waded ashore. All went well until I realized that a guard of honour was lined up along the beach which I had to inspect. Even at the best of times, being an unmilitary person, I do not relish such occasions; but clutching shoes and socks in one hand and with trousers rolled up above the knee, I felt I was not suitably clad for doing the job. The Vietnamese commander was, however, imperturbable and polite, but I felt I had let down Her Majesty's government. Especially as the journalists' cameras were busy clicking all the time.

Brigadier Sidney P. Robertson
RNLI Committee of Management

In earlier centuries people who lived in coastal areas were not averse to taking advantage of valuable cargoes which floated ashore from wrecked vessels, and there are stories of islanders benefiting from some interesting hauls. This was reflected by a minister on the island of Sanday whose Sunday prayer in stormy weather was alleged to have been, 'If it be thy will that ships should run upon the rocks, we pray thee, Lord, in thy goodness, not to forget thy humble servants on Sanday.'

* * *

Some years ago one of the famous west-coast 'puffers' was proceeding from Islay to the mainland fully loaded with barrels of whisky.

The weather was a little rough, and on board as a passenger there was a somewhat formidable old lady who complained to the captain in critical terms that his ship was rocking most uncomfortably. Needless to say, his pride was greatly hurt, and his indignant response was, 'Madam, if your belly was as full of whisky as my fine ship's is, you would be rocking a bit yourself, too.'

Ewart Myer
President, Cruising Association

Sometime in the early 1960s when the International Code of Signals was wider ranging than it is today, I met a young lady in the club with a brooch showing a three-flag hoist.

'Your initials, I suppose,' I said, spelling out the letters.

'Oh no,' she replied. 'My boyfriend gave it to me and it means "I love you",' and she blushed prettily.

Wide-ranging or no, I could not believe there could be such a signal in the code. On thumbing through the fat codebook of those days, I discovered the true meaning of the hoist to be 'Request permission lay alongside you tonight'.

Colin Smith
Second Mate, Merchant Navy

Until recently it was common practice on merchant ships to post a watchkeeper on the foc's'le to keep a lookout for ships. His instructions were to give one ring of the foc's'le bell if he saw a ship to starboard, two rings for a ship to port and three rings for a ship dead ahead.

One balmy evening the watchkeeper sat on one of the ventilator plugs for the for'd hold. There was little activity and he dozed off. The vibration of the ship caused the plug to turn through 180 degrees. He woke with a start to see his own ship's lights only yards away, frantically gave three rings on the bell and dived over the side!

Gerald Darling

QC, Judge Official and Commissary of the
Admiralty Court of the Cinque Ports

A ship is called a 'she' because there is always a great deal of bustle around her; there is usually a gang of men about or working on her; she has a waist and stays; it takes a lot of paint to keep her good-looking; it is not the initial expense that breaks you, it is the upkeep; she can be all decked out; it takes an experienced man to handle her correctly; and without a man at the helm, she is absolutely uncontrollable.

She shews her topsides, hides her bottom, and when coming into port, she always heads for the buoys.

Yacht Stuff

One man, one boat

The Right Honourable
Edward du Cann
Member of Parliament

It was a beautiful day, hot and sunny. Our hero was sunbathing on the upper deck, alone and naked.

To his surprise and horror, he found he was overlooked. He covered his nakedness with the only thing he had to hand, his club's burgee.

'I see you're a member of the Little Ship Club,' said his observer. 'An unusual way to identify yourself, though.'

Donald Trelford
Editor, the *Observer*

A man at a Rotary Club dinner was suddenly asked to make a short speech on the subject of sex; which he did. When he got home his wife asked him what he'd been talking about. He didn't like to admit, to her, that he'd been talking in public about something so intimate, so he blustered a bit and said, 'Sailing – I talked about sailing.'

Next day his wife was out shopping when she bumped into one of his Rotary chums, who came over to her with a grin on his face.

'Jolly good speech by your husband last night – he obviously knows a fair bit about that subject.' Nudge, nudge, wink, wink.

'No, he doesn't,' she said. 'He's only done it twice. The first time he was sick – and the second time his hat fell off!'

Robert Morley
Actor and Dramatist

One hot summer evening, I borrowed a launch from my friendly garage-owner and decided on a cruise, taking with me the friend who normally drives me in my motor.

I have often observed that water 'brings out the bossiness' in people, and the evening proved no exception. I was always being ordered to take the helm or hold on to a lock chain or push off with the boat hook.

168

Finally I reversed the placings, ordered my crew forward and announced that from now on I would take over as captain.

Disaster overtook me as the lock gates opened suddenly and we were on course to ram a large pleasure steamer.

'Go astern, sir,' shouted the crew, and, convinced that I was going to be killed unless I took immediate evading action, I abandoned the wheel and the throttle and hastened to the stern of the boat.

We didn't sink the pleasure steamer but sustained considerable damage to what I believe is known as the prow.

'What I hoped you would do, sir,' remarked the crew afterwards, 'was to put the engines in reverse.'

'Then you should have said so,' I replied. 'When you shouted, "Go astern", I naturally thought you were talking to me personally. You lost your head.'

GO ASTERN!

Hughie Green
Television broadcaster

You get to know people in a marina. Not their names always, but the people themselves. Consternation ran high when word went round that the couple – such a nice couple in the corner berth – were moving to Brighton. Tony Adams, TV star of 'Crossroads' fame, and his lovely mum Wynne Adams, the first aviatrix to win the King's Cup air race, together with other marina inhabitants, organized a send-off party. Small gifts were presented. Personally I thought it was a bit rough for passage but promptly at eleven o'clock the skipper cast off the lines and, with tears in many eyes, sailed the length of the harbour where a large crane lifted them on to a Carter Patterson truck for the journey. Well, they wouldn't need the lifeboat, but they had us fooled.

*　　*　　*

A thirteen-year-old 'know it all' on a motor yacht can blow your mind, and when he's *always* right insanity – that's your insanity I'm referring to – can be close at hand. A sick crew en route to Spain left me desperate in Jersey. Sea cadets on the day of disaster had been invited aboard for an inspection tour. Oozing manners, while they ate sticky buns and drank Coca Cola, I enquired if they knew of an able-bodied replacement for my sick crew member.

'I do,' shouted the brightest of the force who then immediately, still munching a sticky bun, ran off what the press always describe as a 'luxury yacht', shouting over his shoulder, 'He'll be here tonight.'

He was. His name was David White and we've been great sailing friends ever since. But, and it's a big embarrassing but, Nelson junior, complete with kit and sextant, was with him. At 21.40 en route to Brest we sailed off into a mild south-west 2 to 4. Hardly clear of the harbour mouth, Nelson began: 'There'll be quite a swell from last night's blow and we'll feel it as we pass La Corbière,' adding, 'I'd put her round another five degrees to starboard.'

My hackles rose, as he'd told me what I intended doing anyway, but he was polite, horribly assured and, worse still, *right*.

Soon after departure the little lad was offered a nice warm bunk by my housekeeper. This was refused as he'd be checking the log and taking star shots all night. David White gave me a look. A clear night, the beckoning finger of the lonely Roche D'Oeuvres light was soon visible.

'Better increase the engine revs, Mr Green,' Nelson advised.

'Why?' I asked patronizingly.

'You'll miss the tide if you don't,' was the blunt but firm answer.

Pretending not to have taken in the information, I sneakily checked the charts and increased the revs as I'd been told. David at the helm gave me a wry smile. The little fountain of information must be his nephew, I thought. Dawn found us grimly hanging on to everything as Biscay's giant seas caught us off Brittany's Isle de Batz. Picking a smooth patch between the massive waves, we turned and ran for the narrow strait that separates the island from the little town of Roscoff on the mainland.

Safe in the smooth water, Nelson, somehow sensing my antipathy, said to David, 'Have you told him Roscoff harbour dries out?'

'What!' I yelled, adding, 'She doesn't take the bottom gladly.' Then, after a moment, 'We'll hang on the anchor out here and wait for the next weather forecast.'

A grin spread all over Nelson's face. 'You'll have to hang on for at least five days, this blow's set in for a week.'

Day two. Badly beaten, we crept into Roscoff and gladly took the bottom.

Day three, Nelson was due back at school in Jersey, so David and I put him on the rail car that runs from Roscoff to St Malo and watched until it had disappeared round a far-distant bend.

'Drink, David?'

'Thanks, Hughie.'

The railway café affords a good view of the track in case he decided to come back. An old lady served two large Pernods.

'Nice little chap, David. Relative of yours?' I gently enquired.

'No,' replied David, 'I'd never seen him before. I thought he was a friend of yours.'

Five years later, too young to enter the single-handed Atlantic yacht race, our Nelson sailed from Jersey at the same time as the other yachts set sail from Plymouth, beating half of them to America. I'm proud to have had you aboard, DAVID SANDEMANN.

Edwin Boorman
Group Managing Director, *Kent Messenger*

My first boat was an eighteen-foot Thames Estuary 1 Design TEOD. One morning at breakfast my mother started to question me carefully. Yes, it was quite true that four, six or even eight of us teenagers would sail in the Thames estuary for a whole day. Yes, there were always girls as well as men. I thought she was concerned about some danger. I was wrong. The main thrust of her interrogation was to find out not only how the men, but in particular how the girls, relieved themselves.

Imagine the aghast silence when she realized that a TEOD has no lavatory. As teenagers several miles away afloat on the Thames estuary we had suffered no such embarrassment. In fact, after drinking a little alcohol, answering the call of nature often created much laughter. My mother could not be deflected. Either no females were allowed on board or suitable arrangements had to be made. We agreed a drill by which female crew would use a bucket by sitting on the small after quarterdeck, while the remainder of the crew looked ahead.

The following Saturday it was a hot day. We drank beer and wine, and so by the time we had reached the Yantlet channel, three or four hours later, we were discussing the fate of the bucket. The girls at least thought that if the drill was observed just once, they could then tell their own mothers how it all worked. After drawing lots, one brave girl agreed to christen the bucket on the afterdeck, provided nobody took any photographs. With a light stern breeze, four crew members and myself stared straight ahead under the goose-winged sails while Patricia christened the bucket on the small afterdeck.

None of us noticed the *Saga*, the 8000-ton ferry, on her way from Tilbury to Stockholm approaching astern. She took less than three minutes to pass us, close to port, with passengers and crew waving down at us. We saw the officer of the watch lower his binoculars and walk from the wing of the bridge into the wheelhouse, where he sounded three blasts on the siren.

By now the embarrassed Patricia had been completely forgotten. We had been surprised by this huge white ship. I called for somebody to look in Reed's Almanac to explain what the signal meant and what manoeuvre the *Saga* was about to perform.

Sadly, when we had found the appropriate page she was too

small, a dot on the horizon, to show the officer on watch that we shared his joke. All sailors know that three blasts on the siren indicates: 'I am going astern.'

Major Ewen Southby Tailyour
Royal Marines

In 1970 myself and Roger were practising for a race in a fifty-foot yawl that a trusting friend had lent us. We were closing the land at about six knots with every fair-weather sail set – mains'l, stays'l, jib, mizzen, mizzen staysail and even the large spinnaker. In all, we probably had nearly 2000 square foot of sail up.

I went forward to hand the spinnaker. The weather was fine and, stupidly, I was not wearing lifejacket or safety harness. While standing on the starboard side of the pulpit to reach the end of the spinnaker pole, I slipped as the clew of the sail was let free; I had been hit on the head by the boom as the tension on the downhaul took up.

There are enough mistakes in that part of the story with their attendant morals, but as I came to fifty yards or so astern of the fast-retreating yacht, I was horrified to see Roger already climbing over the stern pulpit and shouting, 'Don't worry, Ewen, I'm coming in to help you.'

What I didn't mention was that we were practising for the *Two Handed* Round Britain Race! Thankfully Roger realized in time and set about the rather more seamanlike duties of throwing me a lifebuoy, handing the sails and rounding up to collect his very shamefaced skipper.

Roger and I, sailing in the Two Handed Round Britain and Ireland race in a beautiful fifty-foot yawl, were becalmed somewhere north of the Scillies when a pigeon landed on board. There was not a breath of wind and the yacht was rolling gently in the long swell. After three days of no movement the pigeon moved below and sat on the VHF set which was at the head of the chart table. It faced forward with its tail perched over that part of the chart that covered the approaches to Cork harbour. Although it had steadfastly refused to eat, this had made no difference to its other bodily functions. Cork harbour was therefore more easy to find from the upper deck in the heat haze than from the chart!

This state of affairs lasted another day or so, during which time we became decidedly bored of the pigeon, but we were too superstitious to take any positive action. Roger was below, off watch, lying stark naked on his back in the starboard pilot berth up under the starboard deckhead; he now knows that this was his first mistake. For some unexplained reason the pigeon suddenly decided to take some violent exercise. I was so astounded at this sudden and unexpected activity after so long that I moved from the wheel to the companion hatch to watch. This was another mistake. I was then blocking its only escape avenue. The pigeon panicked and began flapping its wings in short jerky movements and fluttered around the cabin looking for somewhere to land. Deep in its simple mind it knew that it had to look for a branch or twig (or bough, depending on how you view these things), and so it was with an obvious sense of relief that it landed on that part of Roger's body that most closely resembled an acceptable landing site. Roger shot bolt upright (or nearly so, for he hit his head very hard on the deckhead) and took stock of the situation. Without further thought, he made his second mistake. With the back of his hand he swept the pigeon from its roost; unfortunately it was holding on with all its might (and six claws) to keep a balance in the long Atlantic swell. The pigeon left the yacht immediately but the scars, I am told, exist to this day.

Much of my childhood was spent on board my godfather's forty-ton gaff cutter which, in the winter months, was kept on her moorings in St Mawes. On one occasion I refused to climb to the truck of the mast to re-reeve the burgee halyards. I was too young at the time to appreciate that my mother was taking this 'training' seriously. If I had, I would not have disobeyed the order. Without further ado I was bundled into the dinghy, taken across to Falmouth and put on the London train with a note around my neck for the various guards along the four-teen-hour journey. I was met in London by a furious mother. She was handed a note from my godfather which said, simply, 'You sent your son to me to be taught seamanship – he has failed.' I was taken home, washed and fed, and returned on the next train. I was met in Falmouth by an unimpressed godfather who was handed his original note, on the back of which my mother had written, equally simply, 'I sent my son to you to be taught seamanship – you appear to be failing.' I never refused an order on a yacht again. I was just seven.

Barbara Cartland
Authoress and playwright

I never laugh at people being frightened either in the air, or at sea.

I believe it is because Lady Diana Cooper was frightened that I am alive today. In 1924 we were in a yacht, the *Mairi*, going to Deauville and ran into very bad weather. Lady Diana insisted on turning round in mid-Channel and returning to Southampton. Our party travelled on the ordinary cross-Channel steamer and the yacht went off without us, but two yachts were wrecked in the storm that night. Had the *Mairi*, which was owned by Lord Birkenhead, the famous KC, and was never very seaworthy, had another six people on board, she might easily have capsized.

In a cloakroom of the fashionable Embassy Club, I met Lady Diana, whom I had not seen since our trip to Deauville several years earlier. I approached her shyly because she always seemed to me like a goddess far removed from mere mortals like myself, and said; 'I must thank you, Lady Diana, for saving my life. If you had not turned the yacht round that time we were going to Deauville, I am certain it would have gone to the bottom and we should have all been drowned.'

'I was glad to save my own life,' she answered, her blue eyes almost as translucent as the mirror which reflected them, her hair golden as pale corn, her face that of a saint.

'Did you know', I asked, 'that the yacht took three days to reach Trouville harbour and that everything on board was smashed?'

'How thankful I am that we turned back!' Lady Diana murmured.

A story is told that once in a storm Lady Diana went on her knees to the captain of the *Majestic* en route for New York and asked him to turn back, but he refused!

From *I Search for Rainbows* (Hutchinson Publishing Group)

Robin Aisher
Yachtsman

The event was a certain keel boat regatta in the West Country. A well-known skipper of a particularly fast and continually winning boat, while well in the lead and sailing for a particular mark, suddenly realized much to his horror that they had just sailed past the mark they should have been going to. He also had the sense to think that if he turned, those behind would realize his error and get there first! In a flash he told the crew to let the main halyard go. At first they could not understand it, but he insisted that they should do it, and so they did.

Those following behind, knowing that this particular gentleman won every race, and always knew where to go, were not exactly sorry to see that he was in some trouble as his mainsail had fallen down. So they all sailed past, saying, 'Bad luck!' and 'Oh well, hope you make it!' and 'Sorry about that!' When the last boat was well past and they were suitably on their way to the wrong buoy, he put up his mainsail, sailed for the right mark and, of course, won again.

* * *

While racing in a certain regatta in warmer climes where tropical animals abound inshore and sharks and sea snakes are prevalent in the waters, we were subjected the night before one of the races to an extremely heavy downpour. This caused a number of smaller – and in a few instances larger – reptiles to be washed out to sea, among these, of course, being the usual tree rats, frogs, snakes and iguanas.

178

Now an iguana, in case you don't know, is a pretty prehistoric-looking animal, up to about three feet in length, with big, tall, spiky-looking things on its back, and a dragon-like mouth. In fact it probably accounts for the dragon stories from Central America. Anyhow, just prior to the ten-minute gun, the British boat, a two-man dinghy, saw one of these animals somewhat the worse for wear floating on the water. They picked it up, sailed over to the Italian boat and threw it in. The result was electric! Both crew dived over the side, convinced it would eat them alive.

I am glad to report, however, that they gingerly climbed back, found it was dead and were able to start with their boat before the five-minute gun, and so compete in the race!

Sir Rex Hunt
Civil Commissioner, Falkland Islands

As commodore of the Stink Pot Squadron of the Jesselton Yacht Club, I was responsible for search and rescue for the annual yacht race around the tropical islands in Jesselton Bay, North Borneo (now Sabah, part of Malaysia). I had an old eighteen-foot wooden-hulled cabin cruiser driven by an eighty h.p. outboard Mercury. She had been built in Hong Kong and how she had arrived in Jesselton I do not know, but she had been handed down from one expatriate family to another as she was ideal for taking masses of children to the islands about twenty minutes away from the Yacht Club for picnics, snorkelling and water-skiing. It was an idyllic way of spending a Saturday or Sunday. The weather was usually perfect and, if a tropical squall suddenly blew up, there was time to run for home or shelter in the lee of one of the several islands in the bay.

The annual round-the-islands race was a great social event, attracting yachtsmen from all parts of Sabah and some from Brunei and Sarawak. In this particular year there were, as usual, over fifty yachts and they had had the usual trouble of onshore winds in the morning, becalmed around noon and stiffening offshore breezes in the afternoon. Towards the evening, with many of the yachts still a long way from home, a humdinger of a tropical storm blew up. Many yachts were beached around Jesselton harbour and some made for the safety of sheltered beaches on the islands. By dusk, all but two had been accounted for and I set out in *Tiberon* to see if I could find them. I had had my family with me for most of the day. They were salty, sun-soaked and hungry, and decided to stay at the Club. I took with me a young couple on holiday from Hong Kong who had never been in a boat before and were, I suspect, on their honeymoon. It was low tide and we had some treacherous coral between the club and the main harbour entrance. The passage was well marked and I had been through it so many times I reckoned I could do it blindfold. I slipped through safely as darkness fell and the storm whipped up. I searched the outer harbour in vain for the two missing yachts and decided after about an hour that it was time to return. Apart from the flashes of lightning, the night was jet black and I only had a compass and the seat of my pants to go by. Hardly surprisingly, I landed up on the coral. I had a pretty good idea where I was – I had been on coral before – and I decided to drag the boat across it to the channel, whence I knew how to get back to the club. I always wore gym shoes to protect myself from stonefish and sea-urchins and I had little problem jumping out of the boat, getting hold of the bow-rope and dragging the boat through about two feet of water on top of the coral. My ankles were soon bloodstained from sea-urchins but I was quite used to this (contrary to popular belief, the sea-urchins' spines quickly dissolve in the skin and disappear without turning septic). My two guests were embracing in the well of the boat, trying to shelter from the driving rain but laughing and talking and thoroughly enjoying the thrill of it all. The waves were helping me along and, before I realized it, I walked off the coral into deep water, went under the surface and let go of the bow-rope. *Tiberon* came on over my head and I was quite relaxed because I thought I would simply surface at the stern, climb up the steps, start the engine, and away we would go to the Yacht Club. As I broke surface in the dark, I realized that the boat was increasing her speed rapidly and heading towards the South China Sea. There was nothing between *Tiberon* and South Vietnam. I swam as fast as I could and realized that I was not gaining on the boat. I kicked off my shoes and yelled to the man at the stern to throw out the anchor. He later said he had not heard me because of the wind. In desperation I speeded up my crawl until I swear I was going as fast as Johnny Weismuller in his Tarzan days. I was still not catching up. The young honeymooners aboard had no idea how to start the engine or how to get back to the Yacht Club. I had visions of them perishing on the way back to Hong Kong. Fortunately the man had the presence of mind to realize that all was not well and he slung out the anchor. It did not hold but it slowed up the boat sufficiently for me to be able to catch up. I clung exhausted to the steps at the stern before willing hands helped me aboard. I quickly got the engine started, turned the boat around through the channel and back to the Yacht Club. There I found the two missing yachtsmen ensconced at the bar, having beached their yachts hours earlier in Jesselton harbour but not having bothered to tell anyone. There was great hilarity and my two guests told everyone what a marvellous time they'd had. To this day, I do not think they realize how close they came to that night being their last.

I treated the sea with more respect after that.

The Duke of Atholl
Chairman, Royal National Lifeboat Institution

I have only once in my life been sailing competitively, when I was asked by a friend to help crew his *Dragon* as his normal crew were off sick. In some trepidation I went down to Cowes and arrived at the appointed hour complete with dark glasses, straw hat, newspapers, book etc. I was told that all such equipment was not only unnecessary but added to the weight. However, undaunted, I insisted on taking it with me and secured it firmly to the boat. I was handed various rather wet ropes and told to keep hold of them. I was also told that the most important thing was to obey instantly any orders which the helmsman might give. After we had been going for about half an hour, the helmsman suddenly screamed, 'Let go.' With relief I let go all of the ropes: the spinnaker went flying over the side and the boat eventually ended up on a sandbank. I was then able to enjoy the rest of the day reading in the sun while my companions waded around trying to get the boat off the sandbank and rescue the various sails which my too literal interpretation of the command had allowed to go overboard.

Possibly this tale has a moral, but I'm not quite sure what it is.

Basil de Ferranti
Member of European Parliament

My wife is a helmsman in the same class of yacht as I sail myself. I helm number 16 – *Ding Dong* – and she helms number 6 – *Finesse*. In one race we found ourselves both approaching the windward mark, and I firmly believed that I had an overlap, thus giving me the right of way at the mark. She was equally convinced of the opposite situation, and she protested. As we hoisted our spinnakers at the start of the down-wind leg, there was a lot of lively exchange of views between us. In fact, she won the race as usual and, as a result, was able to get back to where we were staying quite quickly. In the general interests of marital harmony, I meanwhile had got myself to the Yacht Club and picked up a protest form to enable her to put in her protest – greater love no man hath!

Happily, though, by the time I got back she was already twenty minutes into peeling the potatoes for dinner, and the chances of getting any respectable housewife to stop peeling the potatoes for the sake of filling in a protest form are negligible, so I got away with it once again!

Roald Dahl
Author

Right up until I was seventeen years old, my mother would take us to Norway every year for the summer holidays. Often, we would stay on an island in the Oslo fjord called Tjöme and each evening we would go out fishing in a funny little motorboat. I can remember very vividly one exciting evening around six o'clock when we decided to go several miles out from land searching for large cod. We anchored near the most famous lighthouse in Norway which is called Farder.

This was in the 1920s, and smuggling alcohol was a famous game in Norway at that time. Alcohol was, and still is, a government monopoly, with a huge tax on every imported litre, and the very fast smuggling boats used to nip over from Sweden and land their barrels of pure alcohol along the Norwegian coast.

Beyond Farder lighthouse, outside the three-mile limit, we could actually see the smuggling speedboats lying in safety, waiting for darkness, when they would swoop in, avoiding the customs boats who played a hide-and-seek game with them every evening. It was exciting to sit there in our little motorboat and watch these daredevil villains waiting outside the three-mile limit.

In our boat were my mother, my elder brother Louis aged eighteen, my three sisters and myself, then nine years old. We baited our hooks with mussels. We let down our lines and began to fish. The sea was very calm. We had a marvellous evening and landed half a dozen good-sized cod. Then came the pulling up of the anchor, which was a five-pronged affair. This was my brother's job, but he couldn't shift it. Everyone in the boat got behind the anchor rope and helped to pull. It wasn't stuck on the bottom and gradually it began to come up. It must have caught hold of something very heavy.

Very heavy indeed. Slowly we hauled and hauled, and as the anchor neared the surface, my brother, peering over the side, shouted, 'There's something on it! Hang on! Don't let go!'

We all hung on but we all managed at the same time to look over the side of the boat. And there, four or five feet under the calm clear water, we saw a large, rusty, iron chest. It had bands around it and knobs all over the lid. One point of the anchor had snagged the chest just underneath the lid. The excitement in the boat was tremendous. Everyone was shouting. Everyone was pulling. Inch by inch we hauled the chest to the surface. Now we had a very clear view of the domed, rusty-iron lid. We could see the two iron bands around it and the spiked knobs all over the lid. The boat was rocking gently in the swell. The chest bumped against the side of the boat, and as it bumped it gave a little jerk and freed itself from the anchor-point that was holding it. We, who were taking the strain on the rope, all fell flat on our backs.

'It's gone!' we cried. 'Oh, isn't it awful! I'll bet it was full of gold!'

And it probably was.

John Timpson
Broadcaster

My maritime activities have been entirely confined to chugging up and down the River Ouse in a rather elderly boat with a tendency to break down in locks, run aground in conspicuous places, and get tangled up in the lines of concealed fishermen. So while we provided a lot of amusement for other people, my own memories of those days hardly merit a public airing. This is, however, an opportunity to explain the subtlety of the boat's name, which may have escaped our fellow river-users – indeed, they were probably laughing so convulsively they never noticed the name at all. We christened it *Manana* – not merely because that typified my approach to all matters of care and maintenance, but because, meaning 'tomorrow', it came naturally after 'Today'.

Billy Burrell
Coxswain, Aldeburgh Lifeboat

A yacht in full sail was passing Aldeburgh in a gale and sent out a distress message asking for urgent assistance. We launched the lifeboat and chased the yacht downwind, eventually catching up and getting within hailing distance. There was a woman at the wheel, so we shouted that she should let the main sheet and wheel go, so that the yacht would come round head to wind and we could put someone aboard. Again we shouted to her, 'Let the main sheet go,' but she disappeared down into the cabin.

She soon popped up on deck again, carrying sheets from the bunks which she tossed over the side. By going below, of course, she had abandoned the wheel so the yacht did come round and we got alongside. It turned out that the woman and her husband, the only people on the yacht, had no experience of sailing on the open sea. He had been overcome by seasickness and had passed out, and she, terrified, was trying to keep the boat going. I asked the woman why she threw the sheets overboard and she replied that she had thought it a very strange request, but assumed it was some kind of signal which would mean something to us!

There was a happy ending because we took the couple aboard, towed their yacht to safety and, as they thanked us and said goodbye, they vowed never again to venture out of the estuary into the open sea.

Chris Bonington
Mountaineer

A couple of years ago Robin Knox-Johnston and I made a deal. He was to introduce me to the joys of sailing and in return I would show him a little of my own sport of climbing. The opportunity arose on a family sailing holiday off the west coast of Scotland in his boat *Suhaili* – the one in which he sailed single-handed around the world. He was to pick me up at Oban and we were then to sail to the Isle of Skye where I would take him climbing.

The trip started badly with me going to the wrong wharf in Oban and only discovering Robin and *Suhaili* three hours later at the other end of the harbour. We set out that afternoon and sailed into the Sound of Mull. It was only the next morning that we hit the open sea between Mull and the south end of the Isle of Skye. Robin assured me that there were little more than a few ripples but to me the waves seemed as fierce as those of the Southern Ocean and, gripping the tiller, for Robin was determined I should work my passage, I turned a gentle green. I wasn't actually seasick but I came very close to it.

At last our voyage was over and we edged into the little anchorage of Scavaig at the foot of the Black Cuillin on the Isle of Skye. It was now my turn for revenge. That afternoon we went rock climbing and I at least had the satisfaction of seeing Robin pause, slightly stretched, on the small rock face just above our harbour.

But the following day was to be the 'big one'. I was going to take Robin up on to the main ridge of Skye by a route called the Dubh Ridge. Unfortunately, I had forgotten the map and was therefore navigating from a twenty-year-old memory of the last time I had been on Skye. There was thick cloud, and halfway up the Dubh Ridge I was nonplussed to come across a vertical drop of fifty feet. Fortunately I did have a rope, which meant we were able to abseil, something that Robin had never done before. I showed him the system we climbers use to slide down the rope, but he didn't like the look of it at all.

'If you don't mind, Chris, I'll do this my way,' he said, and started to rig up a strange pulley system with karabiners and short lengths of sling.

I was appalled. 'You can't do it like that, mate. I am responsible for you and I'm not at all sure that that would work.'

'Well, that's the way I do it on my mast and I don't see why it shouldn't work here. Anyway, I'm not going down any other way.'

And so I had no choice but to let him use his own method of descent. Needless to say, it worked.

Shortly after this I became hopelessly lost and was only saved from complete disgrace when we stumbled on a couple of walkers. I managed somehow to discover from them exactly where we were without letting either them or Robin know just how lost I was. Eventually we descended the ridge safely and returned to the boat. I have a feeling that the score was Knox-Johnston 10 – Bonington 1.

Lynne Reid Banks
Author

We finally had our boating holiday on the Norfolk Broads in 1982. Of the six of us, I alone could claim any nautical experience – scratch-crewing, in my own teenage, on a tiny sailing dinghy on the Thames.

But I knew one thing – one immutable law: steam gives way to sail. And though there wasn't a wisp of steam about our 'plastic launch', we were steam, nonetheless.

Every time a sail hove in sight along the crowded, narrow waterways, I would panic. 'Steam gives way to sail!' I would cry, officiously hurling myself at whoever was at our helm. 'Stop! Reverse! Keep clear! Give way!'

And, albeit with many grumbles, they all invariably did.

Finally we emerged into the broad reaches of the Yare estuary. There one has to steer a course between two lines of posts which mark off the deep central channel. I was at the helm. You really couldn't go wrong – there was far more room for manoeuvre than we had had for days. Besides, despite a few contretemps, we felt ourselves now to be experienced navigators.

I saw the little sailing dinghy tacking towards us. Instead of holding my course, as its captain anticipated, I steered in to the side of the channel in my neurotic anxiety to give way.

The next thing I knew, one of my sons was yelling that we'd crossed the line of posts, which meant we were heading into shallow water. I lurched violently to port. The stern of our clumsy vessel, swinging round with all the finesse of an eleph-ant's rump, struck the poor little sailing boat, and the air was suddenly full of splashes, shouts and curses. I'd capsized her.

What I did then defies all rational explanation. I saw our eldest son tear off his clothes and dive heroically over the side to swim to the rescue. I tried to back up, nearly running him

189

down in the process. Screamed at from the stern, I then executed a half-turn, clouting the upturned dinghy once again and nearly doing an injury to her crew, who, as it happened, were in no other immediate danger. They were standing up to their waists on the mud-flats, struggling to right their boat.

At this point all control of our vessel was lost to me, and all control of the situation as well. I had got the bows pointing back the way we had come. Against the tide, against every law of sea, river and good sense, I struggled to get back to the scene of my crime. At last I drew level with them. Suddenly, to my horror, I saw that we were drifting. No sooner had the luckless dinghy crew righted it and heaved themselves back aboard than they looked up and saw our leviathan looming above them. . . .

At this point my youngest son snatched the wheel from my nerveless clutch. With a few dextrous twists of the wrist, he extricated me from my folly and them from their peril. Soon we were chugging along our previous course, uttering cries of relief. . . . We were several hundred yards down river by the time I realized we would have to go back.

We'd left our gallant eldest son behind. . . .

William Mann
Radio broadcaster

I cannot remember a time in my life when the sea, and being in it or on it, was not the greatest of all pleasures. As a boy I crossed the Channel by maritime ferry a couple of times – both stormy, and by the second time I had learned to refrain from eating a half-pound bar of milk chocolate before the boat left harbour – but I did not meet anybody who asked me to crew on a sailing boat (let alone motor) until the early 1950s, when a neighbour gradually drew me into the net, first with his small ketch, then with an old Dutch barge which he picked up, and we did up, with other helpers and family, until it was sea-worthy and ready to receive our families as boarders.

We had converted this barge *Miclou* from a leaky garbage heap into a handsome boat, and the moment arrived when the owner wanted to move *Miclou* from Rye town (not the harbour, though we did play darts in a pub there with the ferryman who alas was subsequently drowned crossing the tide after drinking thirty-six bottles of Guinness in the pub there during the course of a Saturday evening) to London, where he would berth her at Strand-on-the-Green, a civilized riverside spot. Alan assembled his crew at Rye (we all lived in Kensington, but had this time a gifted galley-artist from the Lake District), and full of delight we set sail one Saturday morning on the tide, provisioned for three leisurely days at sea, and in the Thames estuary. We were half a mile out to sea in idyllic conditions (well, it wasn't actually raining), when our cook told the skipper to give me the wheel and find the crockery and cutlery for lunch. Some fraction of an hour later we were told that we would have to feed for three days on eggs, soup, spaghetti and other delicious foods that we had assembled, in our fingers from their cooking pans. The crockery and cutlery had been left in Kensington. If we had gone ashore, the shops would have been shut for the weekend. Hunger, as well as necessity, mothered the inventiveness which saw us through: we did have to take turns with the pencil and knitting needle which served as chopsticks. For the most part we reverted to infant habits. I have, ever since, regarded my hands as nature's cutlery, and eating irons as a snobbery, though I do try to respect the habits of others when I am not at home.

Steve O'Donnell
Musician

'You always dive with a buddy. Guys who go out on their own don't come back. Learn to trust your buddy and he's got to trust you.'

The sun-wrinkled old diving instructor addressed his class crowded in a small motorboat a mile out of Nassau. The sky was sapphire blue, the sea calm and crystal clear. Ten feet below was the edge of the reef, suddenly plunging to a hundred feet of ocean. After a week of scuba-training in the deep end of the Sheraton Hotel pool we were all anxious to get started.

'What happens if we see a shark? What do we do?'

He spat over the side.

'Normally a shark won't bother you unless it's pretty hungry, but he might take a look out of curiosity. If a shark starts to circle, you get to the ocean floor, get back to back with your buddy and DON'T MOVE!'

This last was shouted.

The water lapped against the hull of the boat, everyone tried to breathe quietly. He had our full attention.

'If a shark's going to attack, it points its pectoral fins backwards and it'll open its mouth. Sometimes it'll rub up against you first, in which case it comes in slow and lazy.'

Hearts thudded, tanned faces paled. Uneasy minds were searching for grains of an excuse.

His eyes squinted.

'If he's going to attack he'll circle three, maybe four times, getting closer and closer. If you see him go twice, start to reach for your knife.' He patted the diving knife strapped to his right calf.

'But you move slow. If he sees a sudden movement he'll come straight in.'

He stood up.

'That is how you go for your knife . . .' His hand crept almost unnoticeably down the outside of his right leg.

'Slowly, slowly . . . Keep your eyes on the shark, keep your back against your buddy. Slowly . . .'

Inching forward, his fingers popped open the fastener, closed round the handle of the heavy knife and withdrew the blade an inch.

He spat again.

'Keep watching the shark, he may be going real fast by this time, getting ready to start his run.'

He paused expectantly.

'Then what?' a thin voice piped.

He grinned in a flurry of arm movement.

'Then you stab your buddy, and swim like hell!'

Richard Yorke QC
Recorder of the Crown Court

The harbour at Omonville has a very high tide range so that anchored yachts may be lying to very long lines. When the tide swirls it is difficult to see where any particular yacht's anchor is lying and any prudent yachtsman takes care in dropping his own hook not to foul someone else's. One evening *Gladeye*, the Household Brigade yacht, was about to anchor, and the captain called to a nearby French yacht in his schoolboy French, 'Mooseer, Mooseer, ou est votre ancre?' After several repetitions the puzzled Frenchman disappeared below decks and appeared later leading a weather-beaten old man in denim, and called across, 'Monsieur, ici mon oncle, mais pourquoi?'

Leslie Charteris
Author

I suppose everyone who has ever messed about with boats has an anecdote of near-disaster; but my first maritime experience outside of large passenger liners might well have been my last.

A running-mate of those days, no less nautically innocent, suggested that it might be fun for a summer holiday to charter a motor cruiser which he had seen advertised and go port-hopping around Kent and the English Channel coast, with selected female companions. Having made sure that we could foot the bill, for maybe three weeks, I agreed.

This boat's home port was at Richmond, and somehow it did not occur to us to enquire if the owner-captain had ever been farther out to sea than Tower Bridge.

We set sail (purely metaphorically) early one morning, prepared to match sea shanties with anyone, and voyaged unconcernedly down river until we were near Southend, when I remembered that another great and good pal lived in that neighbourhood, and should be glad to invite us to lunch and be impressed. So we had the captain drop anchor and take us ashore in the dinghy. He went back to mind the boat, while I called my pal from the nearest telephone. Pal's response was predictably hospitable, and it was mid-afternoon before he drove us back to the sea front to wave for our tender.

What we had not realized, in our blissful innocence, and apparently also in that of our captain, was that just there the tide goes out to what looks like somewhere near the horizon. What we saw was our chartered galleon two or three hundred yards away, high and comparatively dry on a vast plain of mud.

The sun was setting before the dinghy could pick us up, and the disgruntled captain declared that it was then too late to go looking for the harbour which we had planned to make our first port of call. We would have to head back westwards to a marina which we remembered passing on the way down, not too far back, and spend the night there.

Not very gruntled ourselves, we left him to it, and went below to break out some liquid consolation. This exercise went most successfully for some time; until I happened to look up through the hatch, and beheld a very strange sight indeed.

Our captain, letting go the wheel, was silhouetted against the sky, which by this time was quite dark, in the throes of some kind of weird twitching dance, like a marionette manipulated by an unskilled puppeteer. In another moment, he disappeared.

Alerting the others, I scrambled up the companionway, and found him lying on the deck, quite incapable of doing anything useful. Having, it happens, seen such a case once before, I was able to diagnose that he was having an epileptic fit – a malady to which he had not warned us that he was subject. Our skipper was scuppered. And there we were, worse than up the creek, up the Thames estuary, ploughing on without a clue, somewhere or other.

Since I was the only member of the party with nautical experience, having once worked a passage to Singapore as supercargo on a freighter, I was unanimously co-opted to assume a command for which I was totally unfitted. Night had now fallen completely, and at that point the Thames was full of more shipping than I could have believed. We seemed to be surrounded by huge sinister hulls and baffling navigation lights charging from all directions, with no idea of where we were or where we were heading.

Somewhere on the borders of this confusion I was lucky enough to spot what I hoped were the lights of the marina we had been making for, and I turned the boat towards them. Somehow we managed to criss-cross through the paths of all the enormous menacing professional traffic without getting run down; somehow I managed to grope a way to the entrance of the marina without running aground. By that time I had discovered the throttle and located what had to be the ignition key, so that berthing was a simple matter of bumping, pushing, hauling and levering with the dinghy's oars, until aroused denizens of the harbour came to our rescue with wit and sarcasm and tied us up.

And this is the story of my very first command – also of my first charter, which we promptly terminated. It could also have been my first shipwreck. And, as I said at the beginning, but for the luck of beginners and the damned, I might at this moment be trying to tell this story to the mermaids, instead of to you.

Keith Hopkins
Navigator/Radio Operator, Yarmouth Lifeboat

One dark Sunday evening in November, we were called out to search for a speedboat which was missing in the fog. We soon received a message from a tanker which was moored up towards Southampton that they had found the speedboat, which had run out of fuel. As we came towards them and the outline of the tanker loomed out of the fog, we switched on our searchlight to illuminate a very funny scene. The tiny speedboat was lying alongside the huge 100,000-ton tanker. Two men were climbing down the side of the tanker, and one could be seen carrying a two-gallon oil can.

Des Sleightholme

Editor, *Yachting Monthly*

Right at the end of the cruise, three days weatherbound in Cherbourg allowed our charter party to get rid of their francs along with their inhibitions and their hope of a place in the life hereafter. They ate and drank themselves stupid. They trickled back aboard on the evening of the third day, baggy-eyed and ready for bed.

'There's a break in the weather and we're off,' I said. They just looked at me. It was like Hannibal breaking it to his troops about the Alps.

Jock and I got the old schooner to sea and once outside the eastern entrance *Hoshi* lifted her dear old bum in the air and plunged. We had half a gale up the port quarter, and the passage to Chichester was going to be fast and nasty. Down below it was like the morning after Agincourt, or, to vary this military theme, an early Norman crypt, with the stricken lying in orderly rows.

We took the wheel trick-and-trick about. At around midnight I decided to brew us some tea and started for the main companionway amidships. At this point I should mention that we had only one loo aboard in those days, and there was a steady and continuous traffic of groaning Norman Knights to and from it. There was also a member of that suffering band who was a lady of very considerable proportions. To paint the picture further let us visualize this loo as a tiny compartment to port at the foot of the companionway.

I started down the steps. The old ship was rolling spectacularly in the quartering sea. She had finished a mighty roll to port and was embarking on her roll to starboard when I heard a muffled cry. The door of the loo burst open.

Out she hopped, shackled around the ankles. I stood rooted by this extraordinary sight . . . Then, as the momentum of the roll increased, she went bounding across the width of the ship like some incredible clockwork bunny, slammed into the opposite side and – I was speechless – as the next roll to port commenced she bounded backwards across the ship again into the open loo door. It slammed shut behind her.

There was an awful crash of breaking china.

During the remainder of that passage I could have sold buckets at a tenner apiece.

Christina Foyle
Managing Director, Foyles

My father was always attracted to raffish, bohemian characters, and in the 1920s he put up the money for that strange, brilliant man, author of *Quest for Corvo*, A.J.A. Symons, to start the First Edition Club.

Another partnership followed. A.J.A. had a great admiration for a solitary, curious bookseller, Christopher Millard. Millard was devoted to sailing and owned a dinghy with which we explored the estuaries of the Blackwater and the Crouch. To Symons this seemed delightful, and very soon he and my father became the owners of a seven-ton yacht.

Symons had heard that an eccentric millionaire lived on a yacht, moored off Burnham, and made a habit of giving large sums of money to deserving, ambitious young men who needed capital. He and my father decided to try their luck. They rowed over to the yacht in the dinghy and hailed the millionaire. In the middle of A.J.A.'s speech, eloquently stating their case, the gentleman went below, came back and pelted them with coal.

Neither A.J.A. nor my father knew anything about sailing but Symons bought a book on the subject. One fine summer's day they set sail. Symons, always elegant, lay back smoking, with the book before him, with my father hoisting the sails and following his mentor's instructions.

A stiff breeze blew up. The *Centaur* sailed swiftly towards the sea. Suddenly the wind changed and, for my father, everything was panic.

All he remembered was a stunning crack on the head, falling half-unconscious into the cockpit, and minutes later hearing Symons's clear, modulated voice ringing out, "Ware boom.'

Hammond Innes
Author

We had arrived off Omonville-la-Rogue well after dark, and because it was an open anchorage with no leading lights I decided to stand off and on until dawn. It is a small village just to the west of Cherbourg with a stream and flowers and a somewhat medieval atmosphere. We went into one-man watches of two hours each, looking forward, I seem to remember, to an early morning run ashore before sailing round Cap de la Hague, through the Alderney Race, then westward into Britanny.

The wind was lightish, about force three, and it was very dark. We had reefed the main and were carrying stays'l only. We sailed alternately one hour to the south, one hour to the north, our speed through the water barely four knots.

At 0200 I relieved George at the helm. There was a chill in

the air and he was wearing oilskins. As I came up through the hatch he shifted the tiller, leaning back to the roll of the boat, and I saw, past him over the stern, a glimmer of luminosity. I was still half asleep, I must admit, and my heart gave a jump, for the luminosity was spreading, lighting up the swell. It was a green luminosity, and in my half-awake state I saw it suddenly as the phosphorescent glow of some deep-sea monster surfacing close behind us – all those stories I had read as a kid leaping to mind and catching at my breath. 'What the hell's that?' I asked, pointing.

The light had grown, from a glimmer to a ghostly glow that lit the sea, and the air, too. I remember George turning and staring aft. Neither of us spoke.

The light began to change; from all-pervading green it hardened slowly, very slowly, into a pinpoint. And then we heard it, the rumble of a ship's engines, and in that instant George grabbed for the spotlight, shone it on our sails to show them we were there, the night above us filling with a white, iridescent glare. We were in thick fog.

The pinpoint of green, blurred by the fog, was focused now into a hard green light – the starb'd navigation light of a steamer bearing down upon us. It passed us very close, one of the Channel Island ferries with lit portholes here and there and its steaming lights riding high like misted stars. We watched it pass in the fog, wondering why we had not heard the engines, the wind being northerly, thinking how lucky we were that it hadn't run us down. I could see the glimmer of the bridge, and suddenly it came to me – suppose it had been a sort of *Marie Celeste*, the lights still burning, the engines running . . . and nobody at the wheel, nobody on the bridge – nobody in the whole damned ship.

I went back down to the chart table, switched on the light and entered the incident up in the log. And at the end I added: 'What a marvellous opening for a book!' I actually wrote that in the log, and I have it still.

One of the nicer things about being a writer is that everything that happens to one, good or bad, is grist to the mill. That was the moment when my novel *The Wreck of the Mary Deare* began to grow in my mind.

Maldwin Drummond
Chairman, RNLI Boat Committee

Rodel must be one of the most attractive anchorages in the Outer Isles. In the mid-1960s it had changed little – perhaps it hasn't moved on much now. The anchorage is in a pool that

can only be entered and left at certain stages of the tide. The hotel at that time – at least, the part that put up visitors – was very quiet indeed. Right across the front door stretched a gigantic cobweb, which we tried not to disturb as we gingerly made our way in. This peace contrasted violently with the noise of the public bar and it was not long before the crew of *Gang Warily* were part of it.

One of the locals, hearing that we had been collecting winkles, asked how many we had managed to find. When I said, 'Only nine,' he laughed so loudly that his false teeth fell out on the bar.

I was a bit surprised that he didn't immediately pick the set up and rehouse them. He, seeing the question mark in my eyes, said, 'I think I'll leave them where they are for the time being, as I have a feeling you are going to make me laugh again and the next time they come out they might break. If they offend you, though, I'll put my hat over them.'

Keith Wheatley
Journalist

It was, and still is, our first boat, and even then we owned only a third of it. Nevertheless, proud of its shabby sleek-hulled charm, we set off for our first weekend in *Sula*. We were four: myself, Sarah my six-month-pregnant wife, Cousin Zöe, and Harry the grumpy old English sheepdog – a canine Albert Tatlock.

Slipping our moorings at Burseldon Bridge, we headed off down the Hamble in the middle of a hot Saturday afternoon. Our passage plan was modest enough, ten miles round to

Bucklers Hard in the Beaulieu River and supper in 'The Master Builder'. After two hours we were perhaps half a mile down the Hamble, and bulbous wife and slightly built cousin had anchored and weighed five times against a savage tide.

Why did the engine keep backfiring and then die? How did I know? Casting back to scooter-owning days, I recalled something about two-strokes and back-pressure, and another half-hour searching up the exhaust pipe with a straightened wire hanger (all praise to fashion-conscious cousin) produced the offending onion portion. How it got there no one will ever know.

Dusk fell as we chugged on, and so did a murky Solent fog. Visibility fell to fifty yards, and how were we to know that a passing coaster had knocked down the beacon we were relying on? As the sand crunched hard under the keel and we came to a dead halt, barely able to see the forestay, keenness for boating reached its lowest ebb.

Out with the hard-worked anchor once more, and the thankless task of explaining to the crew that there was to be no pub supper even though we were floating off; navigation being impossible. Damp chilly misery communicated itself to Harry and he let out a long melancholy howl. From off to starboard came an answering bark, and as the fog quirkily rolled back for a moment or two, there was a local, walking his retriever on the beach not fifty yards off.

'Where is the Beaulieu River?' we called, for all the world like Captain Cook in the South Seas.

'West a hundred yards and turn right,' came the reply.

And so it was. We just made it to the pub and the family enthusiasm for sailing was rescued from a premature grave. Harry is still not too keen, though.

David Coulson
Deputy Head of Advertising Control,
Independent Broadcasting Authority

A thirty-three-foot ketch is approaching Groves and Gutter-idge's pontoon at a rate of knots with wind and tide under her.

'George,' calls the skipper, 'as soon as we're alongside, I'll need another line at the bow.'

'Righto, skipper,' says George cheerfully – and as soon as the boat is alongside, with crew on the pontoon holding her off, he leaps ashore and trots to a point opposite the bow, with the *entire* coil of rope over his arm.

The skipper's comments are unsuitable for a publication of this kind.

Michael Bentine
Broadcaster and humorist

This incident took place when I was posted in Schleswig Holstein at the end of the Second World War.

'Any yachtsmen here?' Desmond, the senior ALO, enquired brightly one morning.

In the nearby harbour were some beautiful yachts that the Germans had gathered there after looting half Europe.

We knew he was a keen yachtsman, as he seldom talked about anything else. As I had had a bit of experience with dinghies in Dover harbour and the waters off Folkestone, I volunteered. So did two other lads.

Desmond had picked out for us a 5.5 metre class sailing boat whose lovely lines gave promise of great power and speed.

I only knew the bare essentials of sailing so I naturally imagined that the other two lads were experts. Unfortunately as it turned out, they thought exactly the same about me. Desmond, then, was the only one who really knew what he was doing. We gladly followed the stream of explicit orders that rattled from his excited lips and we all knew just enough to recognize what pieces of rigging or equipment he was referring to.

In no time at all, helped by the willing hands of the professional German prisoner-of-war sailors who tended the yachts, we were under way. With a stiff following breeze on that perfect sailing day we were soon belting out into the vast Schleswig Meer.

We made a brave sight as we sailed speedily down the long stretch of shining lake, and at first everything went like clockwork. We didn't, however, always do things quite our skipper's way and he would become restless as we fumbled with some part of the gear while coming about. He started to have real doubts as the wind increased in strength and things began to happen more quickly.

Then it happened.

In coming about, Desmond had seen one of us doing something he shouldn't. Leaping up to correct the mistake, he momentarily forgot the main boom. At that moment the wind caught us unexpectedly from a different quarter.

The boom swung over. In ducking out of the way, Desmond lost the helm and we went aground. As we juddered to a halt he leapt overboard and started to push us off, standing up to his shoulders in the shallow water of the shoal and rocking the ship while we scrambled from side to side at his shouted commands. He succeeded brilliantly. With a sudden swoop, the 5.5 metre yacht freed herself and slid off the side of the mud bank, leaving Desmond swearing in her wake as he tumbled backwards under water.

'Man overboard!' I shouted, rather proud of remembering the drill. Regrettably, that's where my knowledge of the correct procedures ended.

I fully expected a whirl of frenzied and professional activity to galvanize my skilled companions. Nothing happened. They just stood there, stunned.

With the wind filling the sails, off we shot, leaving Desmond far behind struggling in the water. Through his own foresight we were all wearing lifejackets, so he was in no immediate danger of drowning. I hurled myself at the helm and grabbed the wheel as we careered along, leaving our skipper a fast diminishing orange speck on the surface of the lake.

Somehow we got the racing ship around on a new course while one of us kept an eye out for our captain. Sure enough, there he was – a tiny head and shoulders waving frantically. The ship wore round and, gybing brutally, we raced towards him with our lee side well down in the rushing white foam. As I nervously steered straight for him at a good eight knots, it suddenly dawned on me that if I kept the same course we would run him down. It also dawned on Desmond, who frantically paddled himself out of the way as we swept past. Our razor-sharp bow missed him by inches and left him bobbing and cursing in our wake. Round we came again, with the gear protesting loudly at our harsh and inexperienced treatment. Then back we came on the opposite tack – swooping once again on a collision course with our frantic skipper.

This time, as we swept dangerously close past him, George managed to ring him with a lifebelt on a long line. Desmond grabbed it, and found himself being towed through the water, like a human torpedo. He'd have drowned for sure but he had the presence of mind to turn on his back.

Even then, being dragged through the racing wake at eight knots was an exhausting business. Had we not been stopped – all standing – by another shoal, he would have either drowned or been forced to let go. We felt the shoal shiver through the rigging and gear as though we had been hit by a mine but, by some miracle, we were still afloat and in sailing order. We got the half-drowned Desmond aboard and he spat out waterweeds and curses in about equal amounts. Then we set about getting us off the 'putty' which luckily we had only struck a glancing blow. Eventually we refloated the yacht and, much chastened and well cursed by the irate Desmond, we set off for the harbour. By the time we approached it, everything was running smoothly again and we once more batted along, speedily and efficiently.

Desmond's pride had been somewhat ruffled by his experience. So he decided that, as our strange manoeuvres had probably been witnessed by the interested German professionals, we would show them how to berth in style and with British efficiency. We made our final approach at some speed, because the wind had shifted quite a bit. It now lay dead astern, sending us along at a stiff clip.

The plan, of course, was to down mainsail at the appropriate time and coast into the inner harbour, to be fended off by two Germans who were waiting for us on the wooden catwalk that divided the harbour in two. They stood there, holding a long bamboo boathook as though it were a lance; ready to catch us and help swing us parallel to the quay.

We entered the harbour at a good seven knots and Desmond rapped out, 'Down Mainsail!'

Would that we could have!

Despite our frenzied efforts the mainsail stoutly refused to budge an inch. The Bermudan track of the mainsail had jammed tight, probably with all the savage gybing that we had subjected it to. This meant that we still proceeded at seven knots, straight for the catwalk. Desmond was beside himself.

The Germans stood fast and pointed their bamboo lance at us bravely. The hook on the end caught just abaft the bowsprit and the long bamboo pole bent like a bow.

Then, as we turned, down came the mainsail with a rush, completely covering Desmond at the helm. The ship veered wildly and the bamboo lance hurtled back, sending the first German into the inner harbour.

The second one started to run but the yacht, still at full speed and now completely unguided, crashed into the catwalk and cut it clean in half, hurling him, after his comrade, into the water behind him.

The watching Germans must have wondered how we had managed to win the war!

From *Long Banana Skin* (Granada Publishing)

David Coulson
Deputy Head of Advertising Control,
Independent Broadcasting Authority

Clobbered by fog in the vicinity of the Nab Tower, a radarless yacht is feeling her way slowly – very slowly – towards Portsmouth harbour entrance. Lookouts on the bow are changed every twenty minutes or so, or when they become thoroughly disoriented, whichever is the sooner. The skipper's occasional call – 'See anything yet?' – is treated less as a serious question than simply seeking reassurance that there *is* life forward of the mast. But the last time he asked the question on that trip he got the answer, 'Yes, actually. Double-decker bus, fine on the starboard bow.'

A world record for getting an anchor down is pending ratification.

Rodney G. Hill
Honorary Secretary, West Mersea Lifeboat Station

It was local noon, less a few minutes, and we were some six hundred miles south-west of the Scillies, running up from English harbour Antigua and bound for St Mary's. Super day, light westerly brought ahead of the beam by the yacht's eight knots, and the eight knots supported by idle power on our diesel with our propeller wound into coarse pitch. Forty-six-foot Oyster ketch *Morningtown*, main, mizzen and a light genoa set, auto-pilot steering and generally little to do but consider our midday drink and the cold lunch menu. A man in the cockpit, of course.

'Skipper, on deck a minute – better take a look at this one.'

There, about three miles astern, came a rusty bulbous bow, steelwork about fit to set a Taiwanese shipbreaker bidding, and the sort of bow wave a bunker fuel merchant believes every proper ship should have. Bridge hardly visible. Might be good for a try on the VHF.

'Eastbound VLCC with a brown-sailed ketch on your bow, 600 miles SW of the Scillies, this is *Morningtown*, over . . .'

'Yacht, this is the *Monstrosity*. Yeah, come back . . .' (in best downtown Brooklyn, and I change the name!).

'*Monstrosity*. Yes, captain, we are sixteen days out of Antigua bound the Scilly Isles – and it would appear that we are embarrassing your course. What are your intentions, captain?'

'Yacht, we are eight days out of Curaçao for Dunkirk. Roger on embarrassing my course, but as the overtakin' vessel I guess we shall go around you.'

'Thank you, captain, and a pleasant voyage to you.'

We watched that bow wave swing left, then right, then, a bit late, left again, and about 150,000 tons lumbered past, not a sign of humans. Noon had come and gone.

'Yacht, this is the *Monstrosity*. Did you get a noon sight?'

'Thank you for the kind thought, captain. Yes, we are OK for our position, but thanks again.'

'Yacht, did you get a noon sight?'

The penny began to drop. We had had a Satellite Navigator fix come up during the earlier conversation.

'Yes, captain. Maybe it would be useful to compare our plot . . .' We gave him our read-out and fix time.

'Yacht, *Monstrosity* here. I don't have a satellite received and I got me some kind of half-assed noon sight.'

'*Monstrosity*, fine, then, captain. This is *Morningtown* out.'

''Bye, then, yacht. . . .'

Dr Edward de Bono
Lecturer and author

It could have been used as a theme in a James Bond film but it happens to be true. An octopus did shoot at me and came near to killing me.

It was when I was a youngster in Malta. I was going harpoon fishing in St Paul's Bay. In those days harpoon guns had a series of elastic thongs which were used to propel the harpoon.

I had loaded the gun and was about to enter the water. I found that there was no clean way of getting in, so I put the gun down rather than stumble with it over the sharp rocks.

I continued forward. Suddenly I felt something hit against my thigh. I looked down and saw the cord from the harpoon sinking deeper into the water. I turned round to see what had happened. Crawling over the harpoon gun was an octopus of the type quite common in the Mediterranean (about two feet across from tentacle tip to tentacle tip). One of its tentacles had pulled the trigger (in spite of the trigger guard) and fired the harpoon. I had felt the cord tighten against my thigh after the harpoon had whizzed by.

Had I been slightly to my right and a little further forward, and hence deeper in the water, the harpoon might have struck me in the middle of my back. I retrieved the harpoon and caught the octopus.

Lulu
Singer

I was staying with some people in Vancouver, Canada, while on tour, and I went out in a motorboat. It was very pleasant – until we broke down! The other girl in the boat tried to get it going again by pulling the cord of the engine; and I, being nosey, knelt behind her to see what she was doing. And yes! Her elbow shot straight into me. Guess who continued her tour of Canada with a lovely black eye?

Shaw Taylor
Broadcaster

The voyage to date had been faultless. The good ship *Nerina* (a forty-five-foot Osborne cruiser, vintage 1929) had left Ramsgate harbour with the Taylor family on board and, for once, my navigation had actually got us to Dieppe and then on to Fecamp.

We were tied up alongside and the skipper, without a care in the world, was relaxing on the aft deck, pondering on his remarkable navigational feat.

Even the report from the first mate, in the guise of my ten-year-old son, that the loo was blocked failed to shake my ego. 'I'll fix it,' I said. And then I made my mistake. I invited the ship's engineer (my wife's uncle in real life) to help me. Why one should imagine that the production director of a leading manufacturer of farm tractors should be the ideal person to help unblock a loo I don't know, but I did.

There wasn't much room. Both of us top the six-foot mark, and to curl ourselves into the space that housed the 'heads' was a feat in itself.

Vintage 1929 ships' lavatories are a masterpiece of engineering. None of your tiny pump-handle or even self-flushing bomb . . . here a two-foot-long iron rod with a decorated porcelain handgrip operated the all-important pump-out system.

We tested it – it was stuck.

'With that leverage,' said my wife's uncle, 'and both of us pulling, we should be able to blast out whatever is blocking it.' I shouldn't have listened but I did.

In rhythm we grasped the lever and hauled. It was then that I noticed that the short rubber hose that joins the pan outlet to the outlet in the side of the boat was throbbing in time to our efforts. It stretched and shrank, stretched and shrank. I had no time to call a warning before it went.

I don't know if you have ever heard a rubber hose split under pressure but it pings with a high-pitched squeal.

The following squawk came from us as we were sprayed with the finest of sprays of whatever the blockage consisted of. Ping – pong indeed.

As we staggered up on deck my wife, whose acute sense of smell makes her one of the finest cooks I know of, made an instant decision.

'Over the side,' she said, 'both of you.' She was emphasizing the urgency with the sharp end of the boathook.

The rest of the holiday was idyllic – Honfleur, the Seine, Rouen, mooring in Paris for three francs a day – and yet ask the family about the trip and what they remember, and guess what comes out: the day the two four-ringers were piped overboard!

The Honourable H.W. Astor
Director, Hambro's Bank

A friend who joined me in a number of ocean races, after a temporary bout of indisposition was prompted to compose the following, and I have always sympathized with his sentiments.

I Envy Sailors
He stands at the helm, with his mind in the realm
Above. He's a man of the sea –
Away with care! There's a tang in the air,
And the ship's running fast and free.
She holds her course, like a restive horse,
Slipping, shying and slewing.
While I'm on my arse – as green as grass,
With my head in a bucket – spewing.

Sir Ranulph Fiennes
Expedition leader

An old sailor's doggerel from the days before air-conditioning:

As a rule man's a fool:
When it's hot he wants it cool,
When it's cool he wants it hot.
Always wanting what is not.

Richard Yorke QC
Recorder of the Crown Court

Once, on the Copenhagen race, we were becalmed off the Kattegat through a long foggy night. As the dawn rose, on a glasslike sea, we found ourselves in the middle of a Danish fishing fleet. One of us yelled across to the nearest trawler a typical banality: 'Did you have a good fog last night?'

The large and jovial captain placed his hands on his belly and shouted back, 'Alas, alas no. We haf no vomen on board.'

Joan Lowe
Actress

Early one misty summer morning three old men went down to the harbour at Shoreham. They had done this since they were quite young; then it was where they worked, but now, long retired, it was their meeting place. Hardly talking, barely awake, they sat and smoked and enjoyed the warmth of the mist-covered sun.

Suddenly they were alert, almost afraid, as out of the mist emerged the prow of a boat with a long bowsprit, a ghost from their youth. They looked first at one another, then back to the boat as she approached. Unbelieving and apprehensive, they waited for the rest of her to appear. The lines were so familiar, the memories so strong; had they gone mad or died? Was she a ghost? Then they could see the wheelhouse and a young man at the helm.

'She the *Amazon*?' called one of them tentatively.

'Yes,' said Stephen (my son) at the wheel.

There was joy amongst the old men as they beheld the yacht they had known in their youth, restored, mobile and ninety-one years old.

Dr Denis Rebbeck
Former Chairman, Harland and Wolff, Shipbuilders

A great friend of my father's was the late Viscount Bangor. He was a very keen sailor all his life and a member of the Royal Yacht Squadron – but never really in the top flight of helmsmen. He was a very old man when he died and it was his wish that he be buried at sea. There is a small fishing village near his stately home at the mouth of Strangford Lough in County Down and from here the fishing boat sailed with his remains on board.

There is a very narrow entrance to the Irish Sea from Strangford Lough and on an ebb tide one can depend on a 7½-knot current.

His coffin was put over the side of the fishing boat but it did not disappear for ever as was intended! It bobbed up ahead of the fishing boat, heading for the Irish Sea, and increased its lead on the boat quite rapidly. Whereupon one old fisherman remarked to his friend, 'I say, Jimmy, his Lordship is going a hell of a lot better today in his coffin than he ever did in his yacht.'

Index of Contributors

Royal National Lifeboat Institution

Lifeboatmen have saved over 100,000 lives since the RNLI was founded in 1824. They are prepared to face awesome storms and, if necessary, to place their own lives at risk to help complete strangers. Their record of bravery is well known.

The lifeboatmen are volunteers, with the exception of one man at each station, usually the mechanic, who is paid to maintain the lifeboat. They are supported by a voluntary system which relies on local knowledge, expertise and backing to make each station independent and efficient. This system has proved itself one of the best in the world and is able to meet changing demands quickly. The crews themselves know that they have the goodwill of thousands of people with them when they put to sea.

You can help the RNLI to provide the best boats and equipment for the lifeboatmen. You could:

Join Shoreline, our membership scheme
Join your local branch or guild
Help on flag day
Buy our gifts, souvenirs and lottery tickets
Give a coffee morning
Organize a fund-raising event
Collect stamps and foreign coins
Include us in your will

Please send a donation or ask for details of how to help to:

The Appeals Secretary
The Royal National Lifeboat Institution,
West Quay Road,
Poole,
Dorset, BH15 1HZ.

Telephone: Poole 671133